Birding Lite

A Humorous How-to Guide for All
Who Enjoy Watching Birds

"Full of humor, knowledge, insight, and personal experiences, this is the perfect book for the beginning birder. The more advanced birders will see their birding passions in these pages."

Brian Weed, *passionate birder*

"*Birding Lite* is great. It offers an enormous amount of guidance and information. I'm sorry I did not have this when I started birding."

Carol Bloner, *experienced birder*

"I loved reading this! What a kick. It's a fun read for someone going on vacation to a place where birds are plentiful. It would also be a good book to have on the coffee table of a cabin or bed-and-breakfast."

Roger Bishop, *bird watcher*

www.birdinglite.com

May 19, 2015
Jack:
    A friend's
husband wrote this
and signed it for us.
Hope you enjoy it —
        with love your
        cousin June

Birding Lite

A Humorous How-to Guide
for All Who Enjoy
Watching Birds

Stan Dryden

Richard & Anne
Enjoy the birds!
Stan Dryden

Table of Contents

1   Let's Go Birding!   13
    Getting Started in Birding

2   Name That Bird!   29
    Identifying Birds

3   Don't Be a Birdbrain   53
    Whole-Brain Birding

4   Why Are They Called That?   61
    Bird Names

5   Look It Up   75
    Essential References for Birding

6   Getting Up Close and Personal   87
    Optics

7   Heeere Birdie, Birdie, Birdie!   107
    Attracting Birds

8   Seriously, Now!   123
    Birding Obsession

9   The Tough Ones   133
    Difficult Birds

10 Hit the Books!   147
    Continuing Education

Birding Lite
A Humorous How-to Guide for
All Who Enjoy Watching Birds

© *2009 by Stan Dryden*

Printed in the United States of America
by Lightning Source

Contents layout by John Castagna

Editing by Sallie Snyder

Photo of author by Chuck Bancroft
Peregrine Falcon photo by Ted Swem
Cartoon in chapter one by Milt Jines
Other photos by the author

ISBN 978-0-578-04134-6

Introduction

Birds work very hard at making a living, but they usually appear to us to be having a good time – flitting about in trees, "making lazy circles in the sky," or merrily singing. It seems to me that perhaps those of us who spend time watching birds could take a cue from them and make this pastime as enjoyable and stress-free as possible. That theme runs throughout this book. If you enjoy birds but don't consider yourself a birder, it would please me if this book were to move you to accept this "calling." Birding is a delightful, healthy, social, non-fattening avocation. All in all, birders are friendly, environmentally conscious, altogether nice people – joys to be around. But some of us tend to work so hard at it that it has become a lot like just that – *work*. For those of you for whom birding is recreation and relaxation, sit back and enjoy this lighter look at this part of your life.

Light (or "Lite") birding does not mean that there is no learning involved. I feel emotionally and spiritually younger than I did ten years ago because of the many opportunities I have had to learn new things in recent years. In fact, the process of learning new information about birds and birding while writing this book has been very rewarding for me.

I have also discovered in my advanced years that learning is something that comes from within, not something inoculated by others. I hope that the *learning* you achieve by reading this book will far surpass the meager *teaching* contained in these pages. Along the route of our journey there are several paths branching off to the side – some of them well marked and others that even the author doesn't know about. If you take some of these paths, you will be rewarded with knowledge that will enrich your birding experience – and maybe your life. I hope you will.

This book is not intended to be the be-all-and-end-all of birding. The vast majority of the facts about birds (except, or course, for the ones I made up), and advice on how to identify them, can be found in more erudite treatises. There are references to some of these books at the end of this one. But my hope is that you will have more fun learning them here.

The book is written *primarily* for birders in the early stages of developing their skills. If you have been at it for a while, you may find that much of the information in this book is "old hat" to you. But scattered about there are hints that will also be helpful even to more advanced birders. If I think an idea is something that birders of all levels may find useful, it will be high-lighted with this symbol:

Also scattered about the book are **Fun Facts**, little morsels of information intended to amuse you and possibly add to your birding prowess.

Of course, I hope you run across many "aha's" – new information, new approaches, new ways of doing or thinking about things – that haven't been highlighted. And I hope that you enjoy laughing at yourself and the stuffy birders you have or will inevitably meet when you are out spying on birds. All you really need to do to become a successful birder is look at, listen to, and emulate the real experts – the ones that are flitting about, soaring, singing, scolding, and just having a grand old time.

Acknowledgments

I wish to thank my birding mentors, my brother Dave and local bird expert Brian Weed, for stimulating and nourishing my interest in and knowledge of birds and birding. Both are decidedly serious about birds, but don't take themselves too seriously. Instead they take a **Lite** approach to the avocation that includes a great deal of humor and warmth. Both have been my teachers, mentors, and coaches – and have from time to time solved a "mystery bird" for me. And they graciously agreed to read this book in its raw form and make suggestions that made it better.

Friends and family have also kindly agreed to review the *Birding Lite* manuscript, including Carol Bloner, Carole Rose, Roger and Linda Bishop, and my daughter, Sara Dryden. They brought varying degrees of interest in and knowledge about birds, and also helped me improve the quality of the writing.

Sallie Snyder generously offered and utilized her editing skills to help me clean up the final detritus of change after change in the manuscript. John Castagna helped me navigate the unfamiliar waters of book design – it is through his efforts that a collection of Word documents became something that could be sent to the printer.

I also wish to thank Jon Carroll, who writes a daily column in the San Francisco Chronicle. His columns always refresh me with common sense, and the natural humor of his writing style has inspired me to emulate it.

Finally, a whole flock of thanks go to my wonderful wife of 43 years and counting, Gail, for needing me and feeding me though I passed sixty-four several years ago. She also was my reviewer-in-chief, reading and rereading the manuscript and offering valuable suggestions until we finally decided it was good

enough to send to a real editor (Sallie). And she toler-
ated my long disappearances to the "dungeon" (down-
stairs computer room) where I "hogged the computer,"
playing with the words found on these pages. (Actually, that is an understatement – she has been most
encouraging of this effort.) But most of all, she has
made me a profoundly joyous person with the luxury
of being **Lite** in almost every aspect of my life.

Birding Lite

"I realized that if I had to choose, I would rather have birds than airplanes."

...*Charles Lindbergh*

chapter one

Let's Go Birding!
Getting Started in Birding

If you are getting into birding because someone told you that you will see a lot of tits, you might be disappointed.

So you picked up this book and got this far. By my clever powers of deduction, I have determined that something in your past or present has led you to notice that there are objects flying around your space that are neither insects nor bats nor airplanes. Perhaps you have heard your friends or family members, even perfect strangers, rhapsodizing over the beautiful feathered creatures we call birds. (You may even know that "tit" is a traditional term for small bird.) Or perhaps you have noticed birds on your own and want to develop a committed relationship with them. All right, maybe you are not yet ready for commitment, but you are intrigued by them and would like to spend more time with them. Good enough! Welcome to the wonderful world of birding.

Maybe you are already a birder and actually think this book can help you get even more enjoyment out of this pastime. I hope that is true, and that it starts in this very first chapter. One of the wonderful things about birding, like many enjoyable (and frustrating) pastimes, is that no matter how many birds you have seen and how much you have polished your birding techniques, there are always more birds to see and better ways to stalk them.

What is this "Birding"?

People who go out to stalk birds (without shooting them, that is) have traditionally been called bird watchers. That isn't a totally accurate term, because once you find them, what is there to watch? Eating, sleeping, and sitting in one place do not have a great deal of entertainment value. Predators, like diving kingfishers, pelicans, and Ospreys, can be fun to watch, and I am still looking forward to seeing a Peregrine Falcon terminate a Rock Pigeon in a 200 miles-per-hour midair collision. (This rapid descent is called a "stoop.") But often all you get to watch is birds flying away, ducking out

Stooping Peregrine Falcon (Photo: Ted Swem)

of view, or otherwise going out of your field of vision. One might conclude that birds really don't want to be watched – but who does? One thing you need to come to grips with right away is that your love of birds is unrequited. As much as you would like to have close personal relationships with them, it isn't meant to be. So the avocation is really more about looking at birds than watching them. But we wouldn't want to use the term bird lookeratter, would we?

The book *Bird Watching for Dummies*, by Bill Thompson, III, actually distinguishes between bird watchers and birders. A bird watcher, by his definition, is a person who genuinely likes to observe birds, while a birder is more interested in spotting and listing. If you consider the fact that Thompson is the editor of *Bird Watcher's Digest*, it may come as no surprise that the former definition seems to be the nobler of the two. I say potaytos, you say potahtos.

Another problem with the term bird watching is one of image. The stereotype of a bird watcher, as seen in the comic strips we enjoyed in our formative years, was of a person with buck teeth, bad hair, and a hideous-ugly choice of wardrobe – usually accompanied by a goofy expression. In an era when looking cool is a social necessity, you don't want to have people pull that image out of their memory banks when asking about your hobbies. Even when decked out in the latest fashions from L. L. Bean, birders look silly enough, standing around gazing into trees with their binoculars. But they definitely don't want to look like this image of bird watchers!

Sketch: Milt Jines

So in more recent times, the activity has increasingly been called birding. Now this may lead to the question, "Then exactly what do you DO with birds?" But the experienced birder can ignore the smutty innuendo and get back "on message" – which is, of course, that, "I am a birder, and therefore I am cool." Of course you don't actually have to say that if you are wearing your cargo pants with zip-off legs and/or safari vest.

Is birding synonymous with ornithology? Not exactly. Well OK, not at all. This is not to say that a birder cannot become an ornithologist. Verily, many ornithologists became interested in that field of science because they really enjoyed looking at birds – and probably actually *watched* them. Conversely, an experienced birder will inevitably pick up quite a bit of ornithological knowledge – facts about feeding, nesting, breeding, caring for young'uns, and life cycle.

15

Just to set the record straight, let's define the terms:

My dictionary defines ornithology as "the branch of zoology dealing with birds." This unsatisfying definition sent me flipping back to zoology, "the science that deals with the classification of animals and the study of animal life: a division of biology." There you have it – it's a science. It involves the study of how different birds are related to one another, using terms you struggled with in biology class – genus and species. And being a natural science, it gets very nosy about how birds live their lives – what they are like when they are born, what they eat, who eats them, how they propagate the species, and on and on.

You don't really need to know all of that in order to be a birder. And besides, any birder knows better than to use the term "semiprecocial[1]" at a cocktail party. My dictionary doesn't even define birding nor bird watching, but get this! The page opposite the word "bird" has a drawing of a person looking through binoculars. And some people say there is no master plan for the universe!

CAUTION
BIRDING IS HIGHLY CONTAGIOUS AND MAY BE HABIT - FORMING

So here is my definition: A birder is someone who likes to look at birds and whose ability to identify them is constantly growing. One might say that the best term to describe a birder would be bird identifier, but I

1. Semiprecocial: a term for one of the seven developmental conditions that birds can exhibit when they are hatched. It means the chick is mobile, but remains on the nest and is fed by one or both parents. You really don't need to know this, but eventually you might want to.

doubt that the term will ever catch on – at least I hope it doesn't. One thing that often distinguishes a birder from someone who hasn't seen the light is the keeping of a life list, a list of all the bird species one has seen since beginning a birding career. More on life lists in chapter eight.

Birding Paraphernalia

One of the great things about birding is that you don't have to lay out a whole bunch of your hard-earned money to get started. (There will be plenty of time for that once you are hooked.) Here is a minimalist look at what you may want in order to get started.

Binoculars
While you can enjoy birds without the advantage of binoculars, you will find that you don't fit in if you don't have your own pair. But almost everyone has a pair of grandpa's old binoculars lying around collecting dust on a closet shelf, and in most cases those will suit your needs quite well in the beginning. If you can't find grandpa's binoculars, maybe you can borrow a pair from a friend who hasn't seen the light, or you can probably find a pair at a second-hand store that will fit the bill. Just don't pay a lot of money, because some day, if you are as susceptible as the rest of us, you will crave a pair of really fine binoculars. If you do buy cheap used binoculars, be sure to look through them to be sure you can focus on one, not two images.

I realize that some people are not as miserly as I am, and will want to go out and buy the best binoculars available in order to get a jump-start on the cool factor. If you are of that ilk, you may want to jump ahead to chapter six, where I give some advice on finding what you need at a price you are willing to pay. Personally, I recommend against this approach. Until you have experienced the difficulties (and pleasures) of spotting birds in the field, you probably won't be able to find your way through the Byzantine array of choices to find the pair of "glasses" (alternate term) that suit you best. But if you do jump ahead, y'all come back, y'hear?

A few words about using binoculars. DUH! Just hold them up to your eyes, and things get closer, right? It might be that easy when you are checking out that bison in yonder meadow, but looking for small birds on a large body of water or in trees is a totally different challenge. The very act of bringing things closer also does terrible things to your peripheral vision. Instead of gazing at a broad vista, you are seeing only a small portion of it. So before you can study all of the details of that bird, you have to find the darn thing. This can be very frustrating for some people. Here are a couple of hints:

1. Keep your gaze on the bird as you bring the binoculars up in front of your eyes. Most of the time the bird will magically appear inside your binoculars. (Note, however, that this does not mean that you can put the lens caps on your binoculars and bring the bird home with you – fish and game regulations prohibit this.)
2. When looking at birds in trees or shrubs, it's also a good idea to take note of the configuration of the limbs and branches around it, because even brightly colored birds have a way of becoming invisible in plants. It will often be easier to locate the spot where the bird is (was?) perched, rather than the bird itself. Do this with some care, however, as limbs and branches can also be pretty sneaky and look much different through the binoculars.

Bird Identification Aid
The gold standard of bird identification aids is the field guide. (Puhleeze! Don't call it a bird book! Real birders will know you are a greenhorn.) This is a book that has pictures and other information about the birds in any particular area (or all) of the continent. For example, there are maps showing you where the birds are usually found, and totally useless combinations

of letters supposedly describing what the bird sounds like. The guide may also describe what type of habitat the bird is likely to frequent. Many of these books show the different appearances between male and female, breeding and non-breeding plumage, juvenile and adult, and perched, floating and flying postures. There will be more on the selection of field guides and other aids to bird identification in chapter five.

If you are a beginner, you might want to start with a laminated quick-identification card with pictures and names of birds in your area. Instead of the ponderous process of looking through hundreds of pages of North American birds, including Northern Cardinals, Blue Jays, and Eastern Phoebes when trying to identify a bird in California, you can look at a card with just the few dozen birds that you are likely to see in your area of the continent. Although they only show one picture for each species, you can probably find the one you saw in the field before the memory of its appearance fades from view. When I started, I had a "field guide" at home, but used it as a "home guide" – my laminated card went with me when I was on the hunt. This served me for several months, until I realized that I was hooked on birding and would never be normal again.

Means of Making Notes
Most how-to-bird books suggest that you also carry a small note pad and pencil (preferably waterproof, for birding in the rain – sheesh!). This will enable you to write down the names of the birds you have seen. (See the section on "Listing" in chapter eight.) More importantly, if you see a bird you cannot identify, you can write down the "field marks" (chapter two) so you can later identify it in the comfort of your home, car, hotel room, corner bar, etc. The idea is that the bird won't stick around long enough for you to find it in your field guide, so you can talk to yourself (Are you sure you want to become a birder?) about the key field marks and then record them before you forget them.

You might also want to note things that are not related to the appearance of the bird – such things as the bird's behavior, the sounds it makes, the habitat where you saw it, its size relative to other birds (or objects), etc. You can also note questions that you can research later.

A cheapo spiral-bound "five-and-dime" pocket notebook will work very well for this purpose. But the enablers in your family will probably want to feed your habit by buying you birding gifts, and they can find Official Size and Weight birders' notebooks that will make great stocking stuffers.

Some of these how-to books also suggest that you sketch the birds, so you can compare your drawing with the ones in your field guide and, if you use colored pencils, find an exact match. If you possess an artistic talent comparable to mine, you will definitely be able to tell with great confidence that it is a bird and not a warthog. But whether it is an egret or a chickadee – questionable. If you are right-brained (chapter three) and are blessed with a modicum of artistic talent, sketching birds is something you might want to try.

 My dear venerable brother decided years ago that there is a better way to make notes – a portable electronic recording device. Instead of writing down the names of the birds he sees (and generally readily recognizes after 30 years in the business), he speaks their names into his recorder. Being someone who takes the idea of listing (see chapter eight) to the extreme, he can tote up his riches later after he has retreated to a clean, well-lighted place.

He introduced this idea to me a few years ago, and I have become somewhat of an evangelist on the technique. (Perhaps you can sense my zeal – this item doesn't really fit the "minimalist" billing noted at the beginning of this section.) But a portable recording device offers the following advantages over written notes:

1. It is much faster than writing, and penmanship is not an issue.
2. If you don't recognize the bird, you can record your verbal description while you remain in eye contact with it. Those little buggers are just waiting for you to look away so they can disappear.
3. You can even record their call or song, if you are close enough, and compare it with recorded bird sounds (see chapter five) to help in your identification.
4. You may be able to play back its song to entice it closer (see chapter seven).

Of course, you need to be considerate of other birders when speaking into a recording device. As enamored as you are with the sound of your voice, others nearby may consider it noise – a distraction as bad as a cell phone. While I nearly always carry it, I rarely use my recorder when birding with others. For one thing, with others in the group helping to identify an unrecognized bird, the need to record its details is much less common. But I might use it if noting the details of a bird's appearance is a group effort or if the group is engaged in a bird count or inventory.

If you decide to use a recorder, be sure to get one with a digital memory. You don't want to fool with rewinding tapes. Some digital machines have several "channels," so you can record verbal notes on one and sounds on another. Look for a miniaturized dictation device in an office supply or electronics store. The device I have – about the size of two packs

Pocket recorder

of gum – enables me to pause when there is nothing to report, so that many bird sightings can be recorded over an extended period of time on one section of memory. I carry it with me whenever I go birding and use it all the time when birding alone. Rechargeable batteries are a good idea if you use it as much as I do.

Getting Connected

Birding can be done all alone or with a fairly large group. However, when starting out, your learning will not be as rapid if you try to go it alone. You are much better off birding with others who know their way around a bird. While there are several big, showy birds that are unmistakable and easy to identify – like a White Pelican – there are hundreds that fall into the LBJ (Little Brown Job) category. Trying to identify these characters can be an exercise in frustration and can lead to a very short birding career. To get off to a good start, find someone to go with – but how?

You may not be willing to admit it, but you probably know a birder – a friend, a family member, someone you work with, etc. Perhaps it is this person's interest in birding that has piqued yours. If you promise to behave yourself (See "Birding Etiquette" later in this chapter.), the kind birder might be willing to let you tag along. Most birders are secretly insecure about the limitations on their knowledge of birds, and they welcome the opportunity to be the all-knowing one for a change. If you reveal even the least interest in birds, you are likely to get an invitation. If the invitation isn't forthcoming, you have reason to question the quality of the relationship.

There are local affiliates of the Audubon Society throughout the country, and there is probably one near you. Most of these groups have members who love birds (natch!), who like having company when they go birding, and who gain psychic rewards from being the exalted leader of a bird walk. Contact your nearest chapter and join to get on their mailing list. Or they may have a web site with bird walk information and/or may publicize the walks in newspapers, wild bird stores, etc. As a class, birders are fine folks, and you may find others on the walk who would make good birding partners. If you are looking for romance, that is a possibility too, although no guarantee is expressed or implied.

A bird club is another possible source of birding companions, if there is one in your area. These clubs, generally not affiliated with larger organizations, can be either loose-knit groups or highly developed organizations with meetings, newsletters, organized walks, and projects. Their dues are usually nominal. You can search for one near you online, but you need to sort out clubs for birders from bird hunting clubs and clubs for owners of pet birds.

One of the great advantages of birding with others is that you become part of a "multisensory organism" – a living entity with many pairs of eyes and ears. All those eyes and ears can greatly improve your chances of seeing interesting and unusual birds. A birding group, particularly when composed of "golden-agers," can also take advantage of differing levels of sensory ability. For example, a gentleman in a birding class I attend has lost his high-frequency hearing and cannot find birds by their sounds. He has compensated for this inability by developing an unusually keen bird-spotting skill.

Multisensory organism

Did I mention wild bird stores? Yes, there are retail establishments that are actually in the business of catering (pandering?) to people's interests in birds. Wild Bird Centers and Wild Birds Unlimited have franchised stores throughout the country. If there is one near you, take care – it can be like a black hole that sucks you deeper and deeper into this obsession. You will find bird feeders, bird houses (aka nesting boxes), bird seed, artificial birds of many feathers, books on birds, and, of course, optics (binoculars and spotting scopes). The store itself is like the old town general store, where birders congregate to tell tall tales about the ones that got away – the only thing missing is the pickle barrel. You may meet some nice birders there, although the proprietors may not be into matchmaking. Many of these stores also arrange walks led by well-known birders of the area, and these walks provide excellent opportunities to get out and learn birds. Of course, if you (ahem!) decide to buy something before going home, nobody will object.

Most birding communities participate in annual national birding events, like the Christmas Bird Count or the Birdathon. These activities are discussed in chapter eight. Birding is usually done in teams, with very knowledgeable leaders and others with varying degrees of bird-identification expertise. This is a great opportunity for beginners to help in a noble effort and learn at the same time. You may not be able to blurt out the name of a bird, but spotters can be a valuable resource to the team. A word of caution, however: be judicious in pointing out the birds you see. If the rest of the group is intent on getting a good look at a bird seen or heard in a tree, it would be best not to divert them to a different bird that you have spotted. You may find yourself getting the cold shoulder for the rest of the day if your bird turns out to be something very common, or one that has been seen ten times already that day.

Finally, there are adult education programs in some communities that have arranged with local birders to teach a class in birding. Now, for those whose psyches are still stinging from unfortunate experiences with the educational system, these are not classes in the traditional sense – no hickory sticks, no boring lectures, no exams, no teachers' dirty looks. The one in my area is led by one of the local bird experts – he really knows his birds! He selects a different place each week, usually with specific target birds in mind (depending upon the season), and starts each "class" with a very brief presentation to help us identify those birds. Students attending this class learn where to go to find birds, learn the names of the birds seen, often get to see rare birds, and learn how to become a better birder. I learn something every time I go out with the class, and the instructor says that he often does too. (Sometimes what he learns is about people instead of birds.) There may be a nominal charge for these classes.

There are lots of ways to hook up with other birders, so give it a try.

Extra! Extra!

 I learned of a fairly new opportunity to "get connected" during the writing of this book. A web site called BirdingPal (birdingpal.org) provides a "matchmaking" service for pairing birders visiting an area with local birders. When you are planning a trip, you can contact a BirdingPal in that region through the web site if you would like to find someone willing to show you the bird hot spots. Conversely, if you are a competent birder and know the good spots near your home, you can sign up to be a guide for birders from afar and have people contact you through BirdingPal. (Your email address is hidden until you are ready to divulge it.) You are under no obligation, but if the timing works out, you will have a great opportunity to spend some time with people with a common interest.

Birding Etiquette

There was a plan when the Good Lord gave us two ears and only one mouth. People who have figured out the natural order of 2:1 listening vs. talking generally have better relationships with other *Homo sapiens.* The same can be true in your relationship with birds. Although it has been said that most birds cannot hear sounds in the frequency range of the human voice, *The Birder's Handbook* says that is not necessarily so. Nevertheless, the overuse of your mouth while birding can cause you to miss a sound that would have furthered your birding career. Worse yet, if your talking prevents your fellow birders from hearing the birds, it may also prevent you from hearing about the next birding trip (if you catch my drift). Birding can be an enjoyable form of social interaction, but it would be well for you to learn when it's time to converse and when it is not.

Limiting the use of cell phones should be obvious, were it not for the fact that many cell phone owners are oblivious. Did you realize that there is a button on your phone that turns the infernal thing off? Granted, there are times when you absolutely, positively must be available by phone. We are talking about the safety and health of loved ones here, and not much else. For those extreme cases, cell phone manufacturers give you the option of being notified by vibration of the unit, instead of entertaining everyone around you with your obnoxious "ring tone." When you are communing with nature in search of birds, give yourself and others around you a break from the rest of your frenetic life by curtailing the use of your phone. If you must take a call, split off from the group, much as you would if you needed to do some other essential function.

Don't get me wrong – I don't hate cell phones... just other people's cell phones. It is good to carry a phone with you when you are birding in remote areas, in case you become injured and need help. Once you become a proficient birder, you may also want to call a rare bird sighting into your local bird hotline (see chapter eight), and doing that in "real time" makes your report more likely to benefit fellow birders.

Say you are in a birding group and someone suddenly stops and aims his or her binoculars off in a particular direction. It could be a false alarm (you will have plenty of these), but if that person exclaims, "There's a Passenger Pigeon" (extinct), it is probably best not to step in front to get a better look. *Birding Lite* recommends adherence to a pecking order among birding groups that goes something like this:

1. The walk leader,
2. Someone who actually sees the bird,
3. A person aiming a spotting scope that can help others see the bird,
4. Shorter people,
5. You.

Observing this pecking order is generally more important than actually observing the bird, if you want to avoid the wrath and rejection of other members of the group.

Clothing is the last topic on Mr. Manners' list. For the most part, birds are not impressed by your designer duds. You don't need to wear camouflage, but muted colors are usually best. White is generally thought to repel birds – from you and from the rest of your bird-walk group – so avoid it. Some say that yellow rain slickers can also freak birds out, but I doubt that a great deal of research has gone into this assertion. Nylon can help keep you warm and dry, but some fabrics make a loud swishing noise when you walk, raise your binoculars, or make other movements. This can have the same effect on your birdmates as excessive talking, and many walk leaders strongly discourage wearing noisy nylon.

We will touch on etiquette *vis-à-vis* the birds in chapter seven.

A prompt, executive Bird is the Jay,
Bold as a Bailiff's hymn,
Brittle and brief in quality,
Warrant in every line;
Sitting a bough like a Brigadier,
Confident and straight,
Much is the mien
Of him in March
As a Magistrate.

Emily Dickinson

chapter two

Name That Bird!
Identifying Birds

If it looks like a duck, walks like a duck, and quacks like a duck, it's probably a Mallard.

If you are just watching birds, you may not care what species you see. But if you watch birds long enough – mark my words! – your curiosity will eventually get the better of you and you will wish you could name that bird. It won't matter to the birds, but it will to you. Then, whether you like it or not, you will become a birder. So you might as well make up your mind here and now that it is important to learn to identify birds, because there won't always be someone around who you can count on to identify them for you. Besides, learning to identify bird s, like all learning, is good for the soul.

We are going to get down to the nitty-gritty of birding, so get ready for a major brain cramp. The birds you are trying to identify fall into six basic categories, roughly in decreasing order of difficulty of identification:

1. Birds you have never seen before;
2. Birds you might have seen before, but don't remember;
3. Birds you think you have never seen before, but actually have;
4. Birds you have seen before, but whose names are not accessible in your internal RAM;

5. Birds you can identify – either readily or with some effort;
6. Birds you see while accompanied by an expert birder.

Clearly, the easiest way to identify birds and build up your life list is to marry an expert birder. But if you aren't totally committed to the correct identification of birds, you might want to consider some other attributes in the selection of a life partner. I wouldn't think of making any value judgments about you slackers.

The most difficult task you will face is to identify a bird that you have never seen before, unless it is a "target bird" for you (more on that later in this chapter). This task will be the main focus of this chapter. With over 800 bird species in North America, pinning down a bird you have seen to a specific species can be a daunting task. The difficulty is multiplied when those inconsiderate little darlings are not uniform among a species. Appearances can differ because of

- Age, from recently fledged youngsters to adults, often with one or more intermediate stages;
- Gender, if they are sexually dimorphic (That just means the guys and gals look different, but it just feels good to throw around scienterrific terms.);
- Time of the year, breeding or non-breeding;
- Races, or subspecies;
- Variations, such as the yellow-variant House Finch – that one really threw me!
- Mutations, like the White-crowned Sparrow I saw with a long, down-curved bill.

When you put all of these variables into play, now your bird is one among thousands! Virtually a needle in a haystack.

This is a pretty daunting assignment. *Birding Lite* will get you started, but there are several more erudite books that can instill in you the rigor needed to get really good at this. However, as we have pointed out earlier, there are also other, less tedious, ways to learn new birds. Many folks have made birding a very enjoyable pastime without learning how to parse out the sparrows, the gulls, the warblers, etc., all by themselves.

But let's face it. If you really get hooked, some day you will be out by yourself, or with an equally inept birder, and see a bird you don't recognize. So it's good to know the basics of bird identification. If you are new at it, the following will give you a good start. As you progress, you may find yourself wanting to upgrade your skills. Then you can (and should) hit the books written by bona-fide ornithologists (Some are listed in chapter ten.), or even take classes or attend lectures on bird identification. Birding has a learning curve that keeps on rising.

To help you with this, *Birding Lite* starts with some basics of bird identification that will take you well on your way to birderdom. But don't forget what you learned in chapter one about taking notes. There are lots of things to consider when trying to identify birds, and the birds aren't likely to stay put long enough for you to complete your analysis and draw your conclusion. With good notes you can do that later in your car, at home that evening, or after consulting other resources (like knowledgeable birders).

Identifying by Sight

As though the sheer numbers of different-looking birds were not enough to make identification a daunting task, we also have to deal with the indifference of the birds toward our desire to admire them. Those little buggers rarely perch in a place that allows us to study them for more than a few seconds. They are usually popping around in the bushes, and when they alight it is commonly on the opposite side of the foliage. They also seem to have the uncanny ability to sense the precise moment when you get your binoculars trained on them, and they are gone.

Birding was much easier in the olden days. John James Audubon and his ilk shot birds. That made the birds much more cooperative. Then they could measure them and study their plumage to their heart's content. Believe me, even the rankest beginning birder could identify the most difficult species when holding the cold, dead body in one's hands. Another factor in this shooting rampage was that the postal service was in its infancy, so people collected bird skins instead of stamps. Eeeeewww! In fact, many species were driven to extinction by avid birders who just had to have a specimen (or fifty) before the species disappeared from the face of the earth. Thanks a lot, guys!

Bird identification is much like fitting pieces in a jigsaw puzzle. You often have to find a match for several characteristics, including:
- The size of the bird;
- Its shape, or the shape of its parts;
- The colors of plumage and "parts";
- "Field marks";
- The habitat where you see it;
- The region in which the bird is seen.

Let's take these characteristics one at a time.

Size
If you cannot distinguish a hummingbird from a California Condor, you can stop reading right now and take up a different hobby. Size can be a great way to start narrowing the possibilities of what the bird might be. But it is only a start. And there are some pitfalls to be avoided.

The field guides give the dimensions of the length, measured from tip of bill to tip of tail, and wingspan. There is a problem, however, as the birds tend to freak out when you approach them with a tape measure. And it is very hard to tell whether a little bird is 5 ¼ inches or 5 ¾ when you are looking at it from 50 feet through binoculars. A quick perusal of a field guide also reveals that there are several different families of birds that fall into the 5-6 inch range. So when thinking size, think *relative* size. Even that can be difficult when you are looking at a bird flying by. Some birds of the same species (and same size) can *appear to be* quite a bit different in size, depending upon the context – flying high, flying low, perched in a tree, perched on a fence, standing on the ground, etc. But most hawks are bigger than most pigeons are bigger than orioles are bigger than sparrows are bigger than most warblers. So you can start your analysis by noting that the bird is roughly the size of a sparrow, or a robin, or a crow.

One caution to keep in mind: when you are looking at two objects of the same size with just your eyes, your mind automatically compensates for the fact that one is farther away. So although the more distant one makes a smaller image on your retina, you "see" them as being the same size. However, looking through binoculars or a spotting scope flattens the depth of field, and your brain keeps on compensating so that the object farther away looks larger! Don't believe me? Try it. Take two identical objects, like drink coasters, and place them about ten feet apart. Then walk far enough away in line with them that you can get them in one field of view with your optics. Voila! The effect is more dramatic with greater magnification, as with a spotting scope. What does this mean to a budding birder? If you see two birds close together – one you recognize and one you don't – be careful with your analysis of relative size.

Shape
Most songbirds are pretty much songbird shaped, like the bullet points used in this book. And you thought this book wouldn't contain any profound thoughts! Some songbirds might look a bit more pudgy and others lanky, but they mostly have the same classic shape. However, even a rank beginner like you isn't

likely to have much difficulty distinguishing a duck from a hawk or an egret from a gull, even if they happen to be approximately the same size. If a bird has long legs, you can eliminate many species from the lineup of suspects. A long neck is also pretty easy to pick out, and some birds have obviously longer tails. If you get a good look, check out the bill – long and pointy, short and stout, hooked, down-curved, up-curved, and so on. Unfortunately, not too many field guides have birds organized by these characteristics, but it gives you something to work with.

As you gain experience and observational skills, you can look for other shape features, such as the shape of the wings (in flight), whether the wing tips extend beyond the tail (when perched), the relative size of the head, unusually short legs, posture when perched or in flight, and numerous other nuances.

Colors
Color is one of the most immediately noticeable characteristics of a bird. In fact, drab birds are often identified as LBJ's, or Little Brown Jobs. But your eye is easily drawn to the yellow of a warbler, or the red breast of an American Robin, or the blue of a Western Scrub Jay. And the technicolor plumage of a male Wood Duck can make you question whether it is real. Beginning birders are so tuned into color that they think that the organization of field guides is absolutely wrong, wrong, wrong. Fortunately for them, there are some books that let you look up birds by color, much like a wildflower guide.

Many bird names are based upon the color perception of the person who named them. You might think that these names would help you identify birds. But, unfortunately, many of the names can be misleading, as noted on the next page. Some color-based names, however, are helpful. If you know how an ibis is shaped, you could probably pick out the Scarlet Ibis[1]

1. Unfortunately, the Scarlet Ibis is not a North American bird, but introduced from South America.

when offered several choices. Likewise, the Black Oystercatcher presents itself as a totally black bird, although most of its feathers are actually brown. The legs, eyes, and bright orange bill are exceptions, of course. And who could quarrel with the name of the American White Pelican (except for a nitpicker pointing out the black flight feathers)?

You might suppose that a bluebird would be all blue, right? Your supposition would be supported if the first one you saw was a male Mountain Bluebird, but then dashed when you saw a Western or Eastern Bluebird. Here are a few more *Birding Lite* anomalies:

- Purple Finch – mostly streaky brown, with red on the head and breast that tends *slightly* toward purple. Can be quite difficult to distinguish from the House Finch.
- Gray Flycatcher – not all gray, and not that much different looking from a couple of other flycatchers.
- Green Heron – the color that helps me identify this bird is the reddish neck. You need perfect light to see that the dark part is actually green.
- Blue Jay – the Steller's Jay has more blue on it than this bird.
- Golden Eagle – looks brown to me – only the nape is gold.
- Tricolored Blackbird – don't look for something that looks like the French flag!
- Scarlet Tanager – the wings are black, unlike the Summer Tanager, which is all scarlet. But only the breeding males are scarlet – the females are yellowish.

Then we have the birds that are named for their breeding plumage. The Monterey Bay Aquarium has some Red Phalaropes in its aviary, and most of the year people wonder why that gray and white bird has that name – even the graphic for the bird shows the gray and white non-breeding plumage. Likewise, Ruddy Turnstones and Ruddy Ducks are only ruddy colored when it's time to show off for the ladies. (Strangely enough, the Ruddy Turnstone on display, at this writing, at the aforementioned aquarium stays in breeding plumage throughout the year.)

Many bird names refer to the color of certain parts of the bird. A birder has the right to assume that a Green-winged Teal, a Red-winged Blackbird, or a White-winged Dove would have uniformly colored wings, but the birder also has the right to be wrong. Sometimes the green or red patches are completely hidden, and the white patch on the dove's wing shows as just an edge when the bird is perched. In trying to discriminate between gulls, it won't do you any good to compare the leg and foot colors of the Yellow-footed and the Yellow-legged Gulls.

The foregoing diatribe is not intended to dissuade you from looking at colors. Although colors are not as much help as some bird names would suggest, they are essential! When you are left to your own devices to identify a "new" bird, using your observation skills, your ability to take notes (mental, written, or audio), your binoculars, and your trusty field guide, the location(s) and qualities of colors can make the difference between making and missing the call.

In particular, you will want to note at least the following details – your chances of identifying the bird grow as you observe more and more of them:
- The color, including the shade of that color, in terms that will be meaningful to you when looking up the bird. For example: Pink Pearl

eraser pink, the yellow of Aunt Maude's kitchen, the blue of Frank Sinatra's eyes.

- ➤ Where the color is located on the bird.
- ➤ Whether the patch of color is solid, streaky, spotted, blotchy, etc. If not solid, what is the background color?
- ➤ The shape of the color patch.
- ➤ Whether it is sharply defined from the next color, or fades into it.
- ➤ Whether it changes when subjected to different lighting. For example, many blacks become green or iridescent when the sun hits them just right.

Oh, by the way – you will have about three and a half seconds to note all of the above as the colorful little cutie flits around. And soon it will be out of your life forever.

When looking for colors, look at more than just the feathers. The bill, legs, feet, and even the eyes, can offer useful color clues. Gulls are good examples of this. While almost everyone could distinguish a very light Iceland Gull from a dark Great Black-backed Gull, most of the gulls with gray shading in between these two are not so simple. For one thing, a gull may look darker or lighter depending on how the natural light hits its feathers, the background (Does the water look blue or gray?) and where you are standing. So they may not look just like the shade in your field guide. Looking at the color of the legs and the spot on the bill can help you narrow it down. If you are close enough, look also at the eye color. Even with all of this information, you might not be able to identify the bird. Gulls are tough! (See chapter nine) But looking beyond the feather colors just might make the difference between your identifying the bird and it remaining a mystery bird forever.

Field Marks

You will know you are a real birder when the term "field marks" becomes a regular part of your vocabulary.

What the heck are field marks? Many birders use the term to describe *any* visual cue to a bird's identity. Here we will use the term for the visual characteristics not described above. That includes crests (called "top knots" or even "pointy heads" by non-birders) and various small bands of color (You might call them "marks" if you were unusually creative.) that are seen in various forms on a variety of birds. Field marks are particularly useful for differentiating among songbirds.

Crests can take various forms, from the pointy head of an Oak Titmouse to a single feather sticking up, as on the California Quail. (The latter is sometimes known by its scientific name, "deelie-bopper.") Here in California, we are deprived of the magnificent Blue Jay of the east, but we have the equally-raucous Steller's Jay – both have impressive crests. Some aquatic birds have amazing crests usually only seen in breeding plumage. The Double-crested Cormorant appears to be misnamed until it grows two wispy white "eyebrows." The Eared Grebe might more accurately be called the Earflap Grebe until it grows these astounding yellow fans over the ears when it is trying to look appealing.

Here is a short list of the key field marks that will help you nail down the identification of the bird you see – a list that is particularly useful for songbirds. Remember: note the marks quickly – that bird has no interest in a long-term relationship with you.

- Wing bars. No, I'm not referring to airport lounges. These are short bands of light color (usually white) that show on the folded wings of perched birds. The bands are made up of the tips of median and greater coverts, which are the small feathers that cover the flight feathers near the leading edge of the wings. The bands usually appear more-or-less horizontal but slightly curved. If I were a decent artist I would provide a drawing that would make it clearer, but since my artistic talent is indecent, you will need to consult almost any field guide to fully understand wing topography. The point is that some birds have them and others don't, so making note of them will provide one more clue to solving the mystery of the bird's identity.

- Eye ring. This is a ring of color immediately around the eye, between the eye and the feathers that color the rest of the face. It is formed of tiny white feathers, and may completely or partially encircle the eye. While there is great variation among birds, the ring is very consistent within a species and therefore a useful characteristic to note in your quest.
- Eye stripe. This horizontal stripe of darker color in line with the eye often can be a great help in bird identification. It often is seen both in front and behind the eye, but not in all species.
- Supercilium. You may think that this would be a good term to describe the appearance of birders, but it actually refers to something that can help you. It is the "eyebrow" – a narrow band of lighter color over the eye – that you see on many birds. It most often extends behind the eye some distance, but not always. Note the location, color, and thickness of the band.
- Tail characteristics. This may not be as useful as the color cues, but you may notice that some birds have longer tails than others. I'm not referring to birds like the Scissor-tailed Flycatcher that have outrageously long tails, but the ones whose tails are just a bit longer than you would expect for a bird of its size. Some have very short tails, too. One way to distinguish Brandt's Cormorants from Pelagic Cormorants in flight is that the former have very short tails, giving them the appearance that has been described as "flying bowling pins." The shape and position of the tails of other birds can also provide useful clues. Look at the back edge of the tails – are they notched, straight across, wedge-shaped, or rounded? Some birds, notably wrens and some ducks

like Ruddy Ducks, have tails that stick up. Seeing a bird in flight can also help identify the tail shape, as some birds flare their tails while others don't, and others reveal white tail feathers that are mostly hidden when perched.

I told you that birding is fun, not easy. Remember your fallback strategy – start out by birding with others, and eventually you will get the hang of sorting out the nuances.

Habitat

By "habitat," we usually don't mean the classical version of the word – the place where an animal gets everything it needs to live and continue as a species – food, shelter, and the companionship of others (wink, wink). We are talking mainly about just the type of environment where you see the bird. For example, it is not unusual to see a gull on a beach (particularly if you are enjoying a picnic there), but you won't find them nesting there. And, being scavengers, they can be seen dining in a wide variety of "habitats."

You wouldn't expect to see an albatross in a desert, a goose perched on a power line, a sandpiper in a tree, or a Mountain Quail at the seashore. So the type of place where you see a bird provides one more clue to its identification. Field guides generally provide limited explicit information about a bird's habitat, but you can pick up some clues from the pictures. Is it shown floating on water, standing on rocks near water, perched on the branch of a tree, or standing among reeds? Sometimes the common names of the birds provide even more helpful clues. And some guides do provide more information than others. The *Sibley Field Guide to Birds of North America*, for example, describes typical habitat at the beginning of a page or section on a group of birds.

The main thing is just to be aware that you might want to find out more about a species' habitat when you are trying to identify a difficult bird. If you are trying to distinguish between two species that look a lot alike, it might be worth consulting a more detailed resource, such as *The Birder's Handbook* to tease out which one is more likely to be in hardwood forests than in woods made up mostly of conifers.

Region

The geographical region where you see a bird can be a big help in its identification. Almost all field guides show maps of North America (or whatever territory they cover) with colored splotches on them to indicate where and when the birds spend different parts of the year. We don't get Blue Jays on the West Coast, or Northern Cardinals, or Eastern Meadowlarks – usually! The qualifier is due to a little thing called migration. Although each species has its usual places to hang out during breeding season and at other times of the year, when birds are migrating they sometimes end up in the most unusual places. Perhaps their internal GPS went haywire, or they ran into a storm that blew them so far off course that they didn't know where they were. Then they are called vagrants – birds seen where they don't belong. Although the term is not usually used to describe *people* who are motivated self-starters, vagrant *birds* do motivate birders to flock to where they were reported to be seen.

Sometimes eastern-US birds are seen in the west, and vice versa. And sometimes we get birds in North America that belong in a different hemisphere. When that happens and the word gets out, some birders lose all control of their senses and spend enormous sums of money to travel across country and hire guides to take them to see the "furriner."

> ### Fun Fact
>
> Bird seasons are not the same as people seasons. Fall, for example, starts when the birds in the arctic begin to sense cold weather setting in and their food get scarce – around the first of August.
>
> *(The Birder's Handbook)*

The bottom line is, if the map in your field guide doesn't show the bird you have tentatively identified in the region where you saw it, you probably want to be very sure of your identification before reporting it to others. You might instead want to report it as a "possible" sighting. That's the fail-safe approach, one that will keep you from being the object of challenge, chastisement, ridicule, tar-and-feathers, etc., by claiming the sighting of a truly rare bird. We take our birding seriously around these-here parts! But if one of the recognized premier birders in your area reports seeing a vagrant, it might be worth some effort to follow directions to the spot. It can be particularly fun in the company of other birders, either expert or novice.

Once a Tropical Kingbird was seen in trees along a not-quite-dry riverbed near my home. This is a bird that, according to the maps, only shows itself in the United States in a tiny area of Arizona. So I took my waders and headed down there, only to be joined by over a dozen other bird enthusiasts, some from many miles away, sloshing around and forming a "multisensory organism" that helped me find the bird.

If you keep a life list, one way to add to it is to take advantage of the tendency of birds to cluster in different regions by traveling to those places. Particularly obsessive bird-counters travel to specific areas that are known to be "birdy" for the sole purpose of adding to their lists. And you can hire a birding guide if you want to maximize the bang for your time, if not your buck. But you can also enhance your list whenever you travel for legitimate reasons, such as to see the sights, to explore the history and culture of an area, to visit family or friends, or to engage in a favorite recreational activity. All it takes is a little planning, and a little patience (okay, maybe a lot) on the part of your traveling companion(s).

A number of resources are available to assist you in your planning:

1. Regional bird guidebooks have been written for just about all of the important birding areas of North America – Pacific Northwest, Eastern Seaboard, South Texas, New England, etc. You should be able to find one that includes your destination.
2. Birders have infested the whole world, and somebody has probably compiled a bird checklist for just about every national and state park and wildlife refuge you would ever want to visit (and some that you would not). You can find these with a little judicious web searching.
3. Some areas, in particular wildlife refuges, have been thoroughly studied, mapped, dissected, classified, categorized, and described by some person that has clearly gone over the edge, birding-wise. Their forty-page treatises can keep you entertained if you want to spend three weeks or so within an area the size of a large city. You can find these with a bit of injudicious web searching.
4. If you have done the aforementioned web surfing, you probably have also found references to local Audubon Societies and their bird "hotlines," (also called "rare bird alerts") which have the reports of birders like you (or probably even better than you, if you are relying on this book to make a birder out of you). You can call these numbers just before you go (or during your visit) to find out what birds are hot at that time. However, many of these hotlines primarily contain reports of unusual sightings, while you may be looking for birds that are common in that area.

Armed with all of this research, you are ready to compile your list of "target" birds for your trip – the birds you really want to see and have a good chance of seeing. Don't be concerned about overreaching in compiling this list. Nobody but you needs to know how well you did at achieving your goals, and you won't be subject to ridicule for only seeing 80 percent of the target birds as long as you are discrete about it. You can study up on these birds either before you go or on the airplane. See chapter five for some of the resources you can use for this research. If you have any aptitude for identifying birds by sound, be sure to research their songs and calls, too. If you can record them with your pocket recorder you will have them with you in the field. This can be invaluable for finding birds and confirming your visual identification of them. Which leads us to our next topic...

Identifying by Sound

In my earliest days of birding, I thought that it would be really cool to be able to identify birds by their sounds. The next thought was usually, "Like that's ever going to happen!" But, miraculously, it did, and without a great deal of effort or talent on my part. It started with a bird walk with a very knowledgeable birder, who identified a few birds by sound and offered a few tips on how to do it, which are described below. I started a table with bird names and my own version of what the sound would look like in the English alphabet. (This sounds like an approach an engineer might take, no?) But I found after a while that I didn't need the table and was starting to identify birds that weren't on it. Now I can identify about 60 of my local species by sound alone. How? Like I said, it was a miracle. But you might want to refer to chapter three on Whole-Brain Birding for some hints on how it came about.

Of course, you don't always have to identify a bird solely by the sound it makes. Sometimes the sound becomes an added clue in solving the "jigsaw puzzle" mentioned earlier. If you make a tentative identification of a bird but are not certain of your diagnosis, listen to what it has to say. Don't be deluded by the idea that it is talking to you, but listen carefully and try to mimic the sound in your mind. Better yet, if you carry a recording device you may be able to record the song of the bird (along with other birds, airplanes flying overhead, and natural background sounds). Then you can try to relate that sound – recorded either in your head or on your recorder – with one or more of the following resources:

1. The description of the sound of the most likely bird, and alternative possibilities, as represented in your field guide. (As pointed out later in this chapter, these descriptions are not always easy to interpret.)
2. Comparison with recorded sounds on computer software, CD's, or the web. There are also books you can carry out in the field that contain electronics to reproduce bird songs, but some of them suffer from the distortion of puny electronics and tiny speakers. They are most likely to have eastern-US birds, and may not be that useful to westerners.

There also is a device on the market that is alleged to identify birds merely by letting it listen to a bird song in the field. That's cheating, and I condemn its use in no uncertain terms! Of course, if some benevolent soul were to give me one I might soften my position a tad. I have never held one in my hands and haven't seen one in use, and don't know how well it works. If you like toys and money is no object, it might be just the thing for you – if you can live with yourself.

The more cooperative birds (not counting parrots and mynahs) do make a sound that we can describe in our language, and some of these sounds have conveniently been used in naming the birds. For example:

- Chickadees actually make a sound much like "chick-a-dee" (and variations).
- Whip-poor-wills in the east sing "a loud, clear, emphatic whistle" that sounds much like "whip poor will."
- Whistling Duck actually do whistle, but don't try to get them to do a rendition of "My Funny Valentine."
- Catbirds sound something like cats.
- Hummingbirds actually hum. But, of course, they use their wings to do that, not their throats. And one, the male Anna's Hummingbird,

makes a sharp "cheep" sound at the bottom of his show-off-for-the-ladies dive. There have been many theories on how he does it.

🐦 Mockingbirds actually do mimic the sounds around them, mostly of other birds. I once heard one put a perfect Killdeer call in the middle of its routine, but I have never heard one mimic human words. Smart birds!

Some field guides try to be helpful by telling you (in print) what the birds sound like, in a combination of consonants and vowels. You may have noticed that

Sound	Bird
1. zeet zeet zeet to zeeeeee tipo zeet zeet	A. American Pipit
2. ooPREEEEEom	B. American Robin
3. plurrri, kliwi, plurrri, kliwi, plurrri, kliwi,	C. Horned Lark
4. sweet sweet sweet ti ti ti to soo	D. Marsh Wren
5. viderveedeeviderveedeevider VEET	E. Red-winged Blackbird
6. twit-weet twit-weet lilliweet twit-weet	F. Ruby-crowned Kinglet
7. tik k jijijijijijijiji-jrr	G. Song Sparrow
8. sii si sisisi berr berr berr pudi pudi pudi see	H. Tree Swallow
9. reeek trik treet tritilitiliti treet	I. Warbling Vireo
10. tseewl-tseewl-tseewl	J. Yellow Warbler

most birds don't use many consonants and vowels, so I personally have not had a great deal of success in connecting a string of letters with the musical (or not) sound from a bird. Let's see if you are any better at this. Take the quiz on the preceeding page by matching the printed sound (taken from Sibley's field guide) with the bird. The answers can be found at the end of this chapter – no peeking!

Field guides also offer mnemonic versions of bird songs and calls, translating the bird language into English, like the Whip-poor-will noted above. Additional examples are

- Olive-sided Flycatcher – "Quick, three beers!"
- Golden-crowned Sparrow – "Oh poor me!"
- Gold-chained Lecher – "What's your sign?"

One major caution in trying to identify birds by sound: there is a great deal of variation, both within a species and also in individual birds. So it is not surprising that the different species of chickadees, for example, sound different. Just like people, young birds mimic their parents, so birds

> ### Fun Fact
>
> Among the White-crowned Sparrow populations of coastal California, distinct dialects may be separated by as little as a few yards in what appears to be essentially continuous habitat.
> (The Birder's Handbook)

can have many "dialects." Song Sparrows a hundred miles from your home may sing a routine that sounds much different from the ones nearby. And, just like people, birds from different regions of the country have distinct ways of communicating. Some birds switch from one call to another for a reason that is not apparent to humans. For example, the Spotted Towhees near my home sound like they are giving you a high-pitched "Bronx cheer" some of the time, and then switch suddenly to a sound like someone sucking air through the back of the throat. Then there are the birds, like the Bewick's Wren, that have a seemingly endless repertoire, from little buzzy sounds to a very musical mating song.

Learning to identify birds by sound requires that you be even more patient with yourself than when learning them by sight. Based upon my experience, it seems that the memory parts of the brain have a more direct pathway with the visual part than the aural. At least that is my totally unscientific assessment of the situation. When I see a familiar bird, the name often comes to mind immediately, but even a familiar bird sound occasionally takes a few seconds to register. Likewise, with migratory birds that are in my area only at certain times of the year, it is easier to get reacquainted with them visually than with their sound. And it also may take several repetitions of a mating song or call that I haven't heard since the previous season before the name of the bird emerges in my cranium.

Mastery of either visual or audible bird identification through the use of the right side of the brain (see chapter three) involves initial learning and reinforcement by repetition, and is often reinforced by forgetting and relearning one or more times.

Uncertainty

We have alluded above to the element of uncertainty in the identification of birds. If you have been birding for any time at all, you are very familiar with the dilemma of, "is it is or is it isn't?" If you are new to birding, you will soon learn that birds don't fit into tidy compartments, neatly labeled and indexed with an avian version of the Dewey Decimal System. So gird yourself to come face to face with that frustrating human condition known as uncertainty! If your life needs to be black or white, birding may not be the avocation for you.

Now, uncertainty can be avoided. All you have to do is to do **all** of your birding in the company of an expert birder. Then, if the expert is uncertain about the identity of a bird, it isn't your fault and you can wait patiently for things to be sorted out.

But what is the fun in that? A big part of the joy of birding is when "you make the call" – you see a bird you have never seen before and do the hard work to identify it all by your lonesome. What a rush! In fact, there is a fellow student in the birding class I attend who says that he will not add a bird to his life list until he has identified it by himself. Well, I'm not that noble, and I certainly wouldn't recommend this stricture to anyone. But to each his own.

When I was a neophyte at this game I came across a really boring-looking bird. It was all dull, boring brown. This bird was so boring that I didn't even notice that it did have some parts that were variations on brown. Oh, great! How am I ever going to identify a bird that has NO field marks at all? Well, guess what? This bird was so boring that it was in a class by itself – it practically leapt off of the pages of my field guide by taking boring to a new level. When I successfully identified it as a California Towhee I knew that I could do this thing. And you know what? I am now thrilled each time I see one. Not as thrilled as by seeing its cousin, the Spotted Towhee, but I will never call this bird boring again. (Oops, I just did.)

But I digress. The differences between bird species can be very, very subtle. So subtle that, even if you were to use the John James Audubon method of shooting-them-so-you-can-hold-them-in-your-hand, you might still have trouble deciding whether it is bird A or bird B. When you factor in the utter disdain of the birds for your desire to put a name on them, you are often lucky to get five seconds to note everything you are going to get on that bird. Then, is it is or is it isn't a fill-in-bird-name-here?

Let's suppose that there have been reports of an unusual bird in your area. And you charge right out there to see it for yourself. You *really* want to see this bird! And you see a bird that *could be* the bird of interest, but you aren't sure.

So what do you do? Do you take credit for seeing a (fill-in-bird-name-here), or not? Do you tell others that you have seen the bird? Do you report the sighting on your local bird hotline? Experienced birders finesse the question by qualifying the sighting. It's a "possible" or "unconfirmed" sighting. If the reporter is well known, other birders will try to find the bird in order to debunk the sighting and prove their superiority. Just kidding! They are just as excited about the possibility of seeing the rare bird, and they will try to confirm it if they can. Maybe they will confirm it, or maybe they will posit a different theory of what the bird really is, such as a different rare bird, or a hybrid, or a variant of a more common bird. In short, they are seeking **truth**.

A cautionary tale: A fellow volunteer at a local natural reserve thought he had seen a bird that was very rare at that location. This particular bird species has some cousins that are very difficult to distinguish one from another. Another birder, a self-taught ornithologist and much more knowledgeable than I about such things, asked him a few questions to try to document the sighting. The fellow volunteer took great offense at this. He considered himself a scientist and fully capable of distinguishing the differences, and implied that this made him immune to having his observation called into question. But if there is one thing that a scientist is NOT, it is immune to questioning. And expert birders eagerly engage in respectfully challenging each other so that an undocumented claim will not tarnish the records of the area's bird inventory.

Documentation? That doesn't sound like fun! Perhaps not, and you don't need to worry too much about it in the early stages of your birding career. But as you progress, you might some day be interested in receiving credit for a rare sighting on your area or state records. Most states have formal records of bird sightings, and these records systems demand extensive documentation. You can learn more by searching online for the bird records committee in your state.

The expert birder later gave me a sheet that is given to participants in the Christmas Bird Count to document a sighting that might be called into question. This form asks for the age and sex of the bird, the distance from the observer, and the relative size of the bird. It also asks for detailed descriptions of the head, neck, eyes, lores, mandibles, legs, feet, upperparts, underparts, tail feathers, wings, vocalization, and behavior. And it asks about the weather, time of day, lighting relative to the bird and the sun, the duration of the observation, the habitat, and the optical equipment used. Whew! We are talking *Rigor*, with a capital R.

Now this is pretty extreme, and not at all necessary for substantiating the paltry life list that you or I keep. But when there is competition involved (See chapter eight), things get serious. For your personal records, you can be your own judge of whether you have seen the bird you think you saw. Or as they say, "Let your conscience be your guide." The less certain you are of your identification, the more you should try to confirm that the sighting is correct, using the resources in chapter five.

Wow! There is a lot to think about when trying to identify birds, isn't there? But please be patient with yourself, and don't get discouraged. All of this intrigue just adds to the charm of birding and offers countless learning opportunities. You don't have to learn everything all at once (and probably will not, unless you have a steel-trap mind). This lets you enjoy and take pride in your steady improvement.

Answers to bird sound quiz:

1 - G	6 - H
2 - E	7 - D
3 - B	8 - F
4 - J	9 - C
5 - I	10 - A

Scoring key:

Number correct	You are...
fewer than 5	Very perceptive
5 to 7	In possession of a remarkable imagination
8 or 9	Fluent in birdish (birdese?)
10	Certifiably insane

"The moment a little boy is concerned with which
is a jay and which is a sparrow, he can no longer
see the birds or hear them sing."

... Eric Berne

chapter three

Don't Be a Birdbrain
Whole-Brain Birding

Half a mind is a terrible thing to waste.

We'll start this chapter with a quiz. Please select the correct answer to the following question: What is the meaning of the term, "corpus callosum?"
  a) The name of a band whose members have customized hair colors.
  b) The name of a 2002 avant-garde, surrealistic movie that wasn't exactly a smash hit.
  c) A long and winding road through the soupy fog that accompanies the act of living in such a cruel and beautiful world.
  d) The part of the brain that interconnects the right and left cerebral hemispheres.
  e) All of the above.

A Google search of corpus callosum will tell you that the correct answer is (e). But if you chose (d), you are ready to learn how you can enhance your birding skills by employing both sides of your brain, not just the side you are now most likely to use for bird identification.

Whole-Brain Theory

The next few paragraphs may lead you to believe that the author has taken leave of his senses, or that the printer inserted some wrong pages in this book.

Please withhold your judgment, as I hope you will see connections a couple of pages hence.

Many people know that the right side of the brain controls motor functions on the left side of the body, and vice versa. Fewer people know that the two "cerebral hemispheres" control different kinds of thought processes.

The earliest work to understand left-right brain functions was in the study of patients who had physical injuries or defects in one part of the brain. This work began in 1861! Numerous other avenues of research have led scientists to map out where different thought processes originate. Brain scan technology has confirmed and expanded what we know about what kinds of mental tasks make each half start buzzing.

Ned Herrmann, the "Father of brain dominance technology," has been credited with developing a theory in which people develop a dominant mode of thinking preference. This dominant mode often controls the way we think about social and business situations, the activities on which we choose to spend our time, the talents we develop, our careers, and many other aspects of our behavior. In other words – who we are. And it may have a significant effect on the way we do our birding.

The left side is our analytical side – where we figure stuff out. It is logical, quantitative, fact-based, detailed, and highly organized. When we are analyzing data, designing mechanical solutions, memorizing information (like bird identification details), and making plans, we are primarily using our left hemisphere.

Our right side is our intuitive side, where we think holistically and integrate and synthesize information – our creative side. It is also where we process our feelings, and it controls how we relate to others. This is the side of the brain most active when we are being artistic, appreciating beauty, and imagining the future.

Brain dominance theory tells us that our preference for using one side of the brain over the other is rooted in our genetic makeup. We tend to amplify our brain dominance throughout life, because using our strongest abilities leads to quicker short-term rewards. So as we develop we tend to become more right-brained or more left-brained. You can probably go down the list of your friends, family members, and acquaintances and find some who are clearly left-brained[1] -- engineers, scientists, those who always think logically and have little tolerance for those who do not. And you can probably identify others who are right-brained – musicians and other artists, those with excellent "people skills," and big-picture types who have little use for details.

Several years ago I had an opportunity through my employer to attend an all-day workshop led by Ned Herrmann. Before the day of the workshop, all participants were asked to fill out a lengthy questionnaire about their talents and interests, and we were given our results at the beginning of the workshop. Herrmann's whole-brain model has four quadrants – two for each side of the brain – and each participant's results were graphed as a four-sided polygon, with each point at a different distance from the center. My chart looked like a wildly out-of-control kite with the largest portion on the left. I was amazed that I could walk around with my head erect instead of cocked to the left. The message of the workshop was that one can start exercising the parts of the brain that are underused, and build up competency in those areas. You could say that this experience was the genesis of my personal 12-step process of becoming a recovering engineer.

There are, at this writing, at least two online "tests" that you can take to determine whether you are more right-brain or left-brain dominant. The first is the

1. I know this choice of words could be considered stereotyping – but it is shorthand for left-brain dominant, and not meant to suggest one-sidedness.

simpler of the two, but only provides a very general-ized answer. The latter is more difficult to answer, but provides graphical results not unlike those I received at Herrmann's workshop. Have fun, and don't take it too seriously.

1. *www.chatterbean.com/right_brain_thinker/1/*
2. *www.csupomona.edu/~jekarayan/brain/brain/*

Discussion of the functions of the right and left sides of the brain is just one of several ways to compartmen-talize human thought processes. However, it provides a convenient way of thinking about different learning styles. Just be careful about use of the right-brained/ left-brained labels for other people. Even the nerdiest number cruncher uses the right side of the brain at times, and the dreamer who is always generating new ideas for other people to implement uses the left side as well.

Please bear with me – we are almost to the birdy part of this subject.

This is where the corpus callosum comes in. This thick layer of cells connects the two sides of the brain and allows them to work together in an integrated way. The corpus callosum maintains an ongoing dialogue between the two sides so that information arriving in one half is available to the other almost instantly. For example, the image from the left eye goes to the right brain and vice versa, and the brain perceives a single image. If one side of the brain is damaged, the other side may take over and fulfill its functions – although not as well. Of course, everything works better if each side does what it does best – the power of diversity!

This integration of the two halves allows the bril-liant engineer to also be an accomplished artist, often bringing both talents to bear on a single project. Did you know that Albert Einstein was an accomplished violinist? His corpus callosum was working overtime. It also can allow you, if you happen to be as one-sided as I was, to relate better with people who are not like you.

If you are interested in learning more about right-left brain function, you can find a fairly technical review of the scientific literature at *www.singsurf.org/brain/rightbrain.php*. Better yet, there is a fascinating description of "The Great Divide" in chapter two of Rita Carter's *Mapping the Mind*. That book can help you learn more than you ever wanted to know about what is going on in the old noodle.

You may also be interested in reading *My Stroke of Insight*, an account of a brain researcher's own stroke and recovery. Jill Bolte Taylor suffered a massive hemorrhage in the left side of her brain. It took her eight years to recover, and during that time she discovered new insights into how the two sides of her brain interact. It's an amazing story. At the time *Birding Lite* was being written, you could watch and listen to her tell the story of witnessing her stroke at *www.ted.com/talks/jill_bolte_taylor_s_powerful_stroke_of_insight.html*. I hope it is still available for you to see at that site.

So What *Does* This Have to Do with Birds?

I thought you would never ask! Not surprisingly, left-brained and right-brained people tend to approach birding in a different way. Lefties are more inclined to search out and identify new birds while "righties" are more content to enjoy the birds they know and look upon a new bird as a source of pleasure rather than a challenge. But, of course, very few birders are at either extreme.

If you compare the subtitle under chapter one of Sibley's *Birding Basics* ("Learn to See Details") with the quip at the beginning of chapter one in this book, you will see that I have tempered my leftishness a bit here. Left-brained people are likely to begin their birding by studying the diagrams of bird geography at the beginning of their field guides, and remembering the names of the various bird parts that they will need to check when they see an unfamiliar bird – names such as supercilium, tertials, undertail coverts, etc. Then they will create a mental (or written) checklist of key parts to examine and note. If they become very good at this, they will become very accomplished at bird identification.

Right-brained folks will also need to do this, but probably won't do it with as much rigor. They will probably tend to learn how to identify more birds by tagging along with experienced birders, who will do the identification for them, rather than going it alone. And, just as face recognition is a right-brained activity, so is recognizing the birds you have seen before. Lefties may think of the approach as cheating, but what is the point here? Are you trying to polish your resume as a bird expert or to enjoy your feathered friends? The reason righties need to involve their left brain is that they will at times see an unfamiliar bird that they would really like to identify without the benefit of someone who either knows it or has the checklist routine down cold. Of course that doesn't matter if they are really hard-core right-brainers – they may not even need to identify the birds to enjoy them.

Rather than either/or, think of the variety of left- and right-brain activities that different people employ, or one person employs at different times, as a continuum. Consider the following list of things you might be doing as you are out pursuing our feathered friends. They progress from right-brained to left, and may even describe the stages of development of an obsessive/compulsive birder:

1. Close your eyes and listen – gift from God, feast for the right brain.
2. Start to wonder about what kinds of birds you hear and see.
3. Make a note of a few characteristics so you can ask someone.

4. Make a note of field marks so you can look the bird up yourself.
5. Experience the "rush" when you identify a difficult bird by yourself for the first time.
6. Start keeping track of the birds you see.
7. Create a life list, then other lists – monthly, birds in your yard, county, etc.
8. Get into competitive birding, where it is necessary to document your findings.

In business, social, and personal relationships, things do not always go smoothly between left-brained and right-brained people. As a left-brainer, I have been known to show impatience with those who are "always chasing rainbows." They keep coming up with these supposedly great ideas, but the ideas are not always well thought out, and those who conceive ideas often want someone else to implement them. The righties have been disappointed when I dashed cold water on their ideas, and sometimes thought of me as a "negative person." (This is so unfair. They only felt that way because it was true.) This sort of dissonance can also exist in the wonderful world of birding. Serious birders, hot on the trail of a rare water bird, may question your credentials when you exclaim on the sighting of a commonplace bird – a Cinnamon Teal, for instance. But if your heart doesn't take a little leap each time you see a breeding male Cinnamon Teal, then you probably aren't using your right brain enough. You can find out what I mean about this bird by going to the home page of the *Birding Lite* web site, *www.birdinglite.com*.

The bottom line on all this right-left brain theory as it applies to birding is this – you need to use both sides in order to be a really fine birder. You may identify birds you are already familiar with by noticing all sorts of characteristics and behaviors that may be difficult to describe in words – posture when perched, flight patterns, how they sit in the water, speed and shape of the wingbeats, behavior on the ground, a pattern on the underside of the wings, vocalization, and on and on. These things allow you to identify birds in a fraction of a second and knock the socks off of beginners who will wonder how you do it (and maybe suspect you are making stuff up). And just like recognizing a familiar face, it's the right side of your brain that is making this happen.

But what happens if you see a bird you have never seen before, or one that you have only seen once or twice, or a variant of one you have seen many times? That's when you have to get the left side in gear. You need to have developed the knowledge of bird geography so you can make mental notes about the various shapes and colors and "hit the books" to identify the bird. So this is where Sibley's exhortation to "learn to see details" pays off.

You may have detected a bias in the foregoing towards preferring the right side for birding. Part of this may be rebound (or penance) for being such a leftie for the majority of my life. But personally I find the identification of familiar birds to be a somewhat more satisfying part of birding because, let's face it, if you do most of your birding within twenty miles of home you are going to see many, many more familiar birds than newbies. But I have to admit that on the rare occasions when I spot a new bird and do the hard work of identifying it, I am pretty proud of myself. And I also suspect that I have at times missed identifying a new bird because it looked like a familiar bird and I just got sloppy and failed to engage my left side. Try not to do that.

> "I once had a sparrow alight upon my shoulder for a moment, while I was hoeing in a village garden, and I felt that I was more distinguished by that circumstance that I should have been by any epaulet I could have worn."
>
> ...Henry David Thoreau

chapter four

Why Are They Called That?
Bird Names

> *What's in a name? That which we call*
> *a Rose-breasted Grosbeak by any other*
> *name would sound as sweet.*

What's in a name? For a birder, knowing what to call the bird you just saw is what it's all about. I don't mean a name like Tweety, or Britney, or Clarence, but the name that identifies the species. Notice I didn't write "the name that *describes* the species." Each individual bird species is identified by one (or more) common name(s), and we'll get to that bit of confusion later.

I must admit that I was a bit intimidated by all those bird names when starting out in birding. I just could not understand what that eclectic collection of names was all about. There must have been some mysterious logic behind it that I could not comprehend. This chapter is intended to put your mind at ease over the need (or lack thereof) to understand the system.

Just like other animals and plants, birds have two-part scientific names that identify the genus and species of each bird. You generally don't need to bother yourself with these names (at least in the early stages of your birderhood), although you may run into snobbish birders who will try to impress you with their Latin. Humor them if you wish, but don't let them intimidate you. Perhaps you would be mightily impressed with someone identifying a *Passerina cyanea*, but wouldn't you also be pretty impressed with an Indigo Bunting – the bird itself, if not the birder? Besides, while Latin is the predominant source of the scientific names, Greek and other languages have crept in, so your snooty scientific name-spewer is actually speaking a mongrelized language. But don't tell that person – Miss Manners wouldn't approve. By the way, *Scientific names* are always *italicized* and always *Capitalized uniformly*.

Unlike plants, with birds there is a fairly uniform system of common names. But it hasn't always been that way. In the good ol' days of birding, people were inventing birds (or maybe just their names) right and left, and may not have realized that someone in another area had already seen and named it. So, of course, the ornithologist gave it whatever name struck his[1] fancy. It has been estimated that there were at one time about a half-million common bird names in use. Through the monumental efforts of the American Ornithologists' Union in creating the fifth edition of the *Check-list of North American Birds* in 1957, there is now just one commonly accepted name for each species. So now a White-crowned Sparrow is never called a White-stripey-headed Sparrow, even though that might describe the bird more accurately.

> ## *Fun Fact*
> Former names for Great Blue Heron:
> Big Cranky
> Blue Crane
> Poor Joe

If you want to read all the gory details of the process of naming birds, I direct you to *The Dictionary of American Bird Names*, by Ernest Choate. The most recent "Revised Edition" was published in 1985 and is out of print, but it is still available from online sources (for prices ranging from under $10 to over $100 – go figure!). Don't think for one moment that the gurus who created the unified list of bird names could leave well enough alone. Oh, no! Common names are continu-

---

1. Note that I did not use the so-called correct "his or her" in this context. In those days if someone was a scientist, it was almost certainly a man.

ally becoming New! and Improved! The experts are continually arguing over "splitting" one species into two, or "lumping" two or more into one. The development of DNA testing has given them unlimited power to meddle with bird species. So we are dealing with a moving target here, and this book was probably out of date a week after it was published. But I can guarantee that you will learn more about bird naming from Choate's book than you ever wanted to know.

Watch out for those name changes, though. People still use Rufous-sided Towhee (and who can blame them?), although the bird-naming police banned that exquisite name several years ago when they decided that the Spotted Towhee of the west and the Eastern Towhee were different species.

A few words about capitalization. There seem to be several schools of thought on this, from those who capitalize every word in the name to those who don't capitalize any of them. The convention that seems to be the most commonly used is to capitalize each word except a hyphenated suffix – for example Black-headed Grosbeak.[2] It had been my habit to only capitalize the first word of the name (following the convention of Scientific names), but after extensive research (which took me a whole three minutes) in the resources at my disposal I am hereby repenting my wicked ways and will henceforth use the more common style. If you see that I have failed to do so anywhere in this book, feel free to use my name in vain. However, you should be aware of one immutable fact: the birds don't care! This is because: a) they are pretty laid back, and b) they can't read. Additionally, when writing of families of birds (for example, flycatchers), instead of a distinct species, it is common not to capitalize at all.

---

2. In a few hyphenated bird names the suffix is also capitalized, as in Western Scrub-Jay and its kin. Also, some sources hyphenate Whistling-Duck, while others don't. Don't ask why.

One thing you might notice is that there doesn't seem to be any rhyme or reason to how common bird names have been handed out. Within a family of birds, the individual species have been given common names based on their appearance, their behavior, or their region or habitat – or they have some dude's (or dudette's) surname attached to them. Clearly, this chaos cannot continue! Therefore I am proud to announce the newly-invented

Birding Lite **System of Classification of Common Bird Names**

This system consists of the following categories:
1. Names that describe the appearance of the birds
2. Names that describe the behavior of the birds
3. Names that describe the sounds the birds make
4. Names that describe where the birds can be found
5. Unpronounceable names
6. Names that are just plain wrong
7. Names that seem wrong, but are really accurate
8. Names that aggrandize the persons naming the birds (or someone else)
9. Names with fascinating derivations
10. The rest

The following discussion of each category includes examples of the birds in each one.

1. Names that describe the appearance of the birds
    - Great Blue Heron
    - Black-capped Chickadee
    - Red Phalarope
    - Red-tailed Hawk

This seems to be a pretty straightforward way of naming something. It would certainly make birding easier if one could use a name that described the bird. However, it isn't so simple, because many different species look very much alike. On further review, then, the names of the birds mentioned above are not always adequate.

64

- Size is relative. There is a bird called the Little Blue Heron, which, while smaller than its "Great" cousin, is not exactly the size of a wren.
- Birds may have similarities as well as differences in appearance. The head of a Chestnut-backed Chickadee looks very much like that of his cousin, who was in line ahead of him to get the Black-capped name.
- Some birds change with the seasons. The Red Phalarope is only (mostly) red during the breeding season – in the winter it's varying shades of gray.
- Other birds look different when they are youngsters. The juvenile Red-tailed Hawk isn't red-tailed.

Some birds are so bizarre-looking that they defy description. The Harlequin Duck is aptly named, but the Wood Duck is even more outrageous in appearance and has a pedestrian name.

2. Names that describe the behavior of the birds
- Blue-gray Gnatcatcher
- Black Skimmer
- Acorn Woodpecker
- Kingfishers
- Turnstones
- Sapsuckers
- American Dipper
- Townsend's Solitaire

Here we are primarily talking about the birds' eating habits – what they eat and how they eat. Most of these names, however, are not exclusive. Gnatcatchers and flycatchers eat mostly flying insects, but they are not limited to gnats and flies, respectively. Both may go after a tasty insect that is perched on a plant. And they are by no means the only birds that catch insects in mid-air – swallows and swifts are the most impressive foragers of small flying critters.

Some names are very descriptive of the manner of eating. The Black Skimmer, for example, is specially adapted with an elongated lower mandible to skim along the water picking up small fish and crustaceans. Some terns have been seen doing this, but generally they are kerplunkers rather than skimmers.

Turnstones also get their names from unusual habits – turning over stones to find food. Again, however, that is not their only means of foraging. The Black Turnstones along the rocky west coast more commonly are seen on intertidal rocks where the wave action precludes the presence of loose stones, and there they don't have the opportunity to live up to their name. They don't seem to be the least bit embarrassed by this, either.

You will be glad to know that the American Dipper's name refers to foraging behavior, not tobacco use. The name actually describes two kinds of dipping. Sometimes they sit on streamside rocks and dip their bill to glean insects from the water's surface. But they also "take a dip" (go under water) to search for food. *The Birder's Handbook* offers the Fun Fact to the right, but is silent on whether these birds spit after they dip.

> ## Fun Fact
>
> regarding American Dippers: "Amazingly, these birds are able to forage on the bottom of streams in which the current is too fast and the water too deep for people to stand."
> (*The Birder's Handbook*)

There are several bird behaviors that are not related to food. You would probably never guess how the wagtails get their names, so I'll tell you – they "wag" their tails! Actually, many field guides admit that it is not wagging in the canine sense, but more of an up and down pumping action. Once again, these birds are joined in this suggestive behavior by others – their relatives, the pipits, and phoebes too. The Spotted Sandpiper and the Wandering Tattler are the national co-champions in this regard; if you see a bird land on a rock 100 yards away and furiously pump its tail, it is most likely one or the other of these guys.

The Townsend's Solitaire is aptly named for its elusive habits. Like Greta Garbo, it "vants" to be alone.

Other behaviors reflected in bird names have to do with nesting behavior. Burrowing Owls, for example, nest in the burrows of mammals, often enlarging them by kicking dirt backward. Chimney Swifts are also aptly named, as they often build their nests in abandoned chimneys and other human structures with an opening at the top. The nest is made of twigs that are glued to each other, and to a vertical wall, with saliva. (I don't know if they dip.) Butbutbutbutbut... you may ask, "Where did they nest before humans were around to build chimneys?" In early days, humans also weren't around to cut down old hollow trees, and they made fine prehistoric chimneys. People weren't around to name them Hollow-tree Swifts either.

> **Fun Fact**
>
> Swifts cannot perch on horizontal surfaces, but can cling to vertical walls.

The behavior-based name of the Greater Roadrunner is slightly misleading. They often streak across fields in search of food or to escape predators, such as Wile E. Coyote. Their name, I suppose, comes from the fact that they are easier to spot when running down roads.

3. Names that describe the sounds the birds make
   - Northern Mockingbird
   - Chickadees
   - Whip-poor-will (and kin)
   - Whistling Ducks
   - Laughing Gull
   - Gray Catbird
   - Hummingbirds

This takes a little imagination and use of the right side of the brain. The mockingbirds are aptly named because their long and varied songs often include mimicry of other birds, or sometimes other sounds.

In California we have the Chestnut-backed Chickadee, and the name works for me. The Black-capped Chickadees in Oregon, though, might be more appropriately named Chickadeedeedees – that is the sound they make. Oak Titmice (Titmouses?) can also make a chick-a-dee sound, but they sound like they have a serious head cold. Nevertheless, they claim family rights to the sound, because they are related to chickadees.

I have not had the opportunity to judge the naming accuracy of some of the birds below in person, but the recordings on *Thayer's Birding Software* suggest to me the following:

- Whip-poor-will might be changed to Whip-poor-wheep.
- Common Poor-will might be changed to Common Poor-gloogle.
- Chuck-will's Widow is a bit of a stretch, but I'll buy it.
- Whistling Ducks could be called Squeaking Ducks.
- Laughing Gull works for me.
- Catbird? Puhleeze!

Somebody must have had it in for ol' Will. They wanted him to be either poor or dead.

Hummingbirds don't hum vocally, but with their wings. They also make vocal sounds, but it would take some wild imagination to name them from those sounds. And since the various species are obviously related, humming is a good way to describe them. But the hums are not all the same. Anna's Hummingbirds, when they come up behind one in the garden, sound like giant bumblebees. The Allen's Hummingbirds, which visit my area in the spring, make a whirring sound like tiny turbines as they streak by, but the name Whirlybird was already taken by a much larger species.

4. Names that describe where the birds can be found
  - 🐦 Northern Harrier/Shrike/Fulmar/Etceteras
  - 🐦 American Robin
  - 🐦 California Towhee
  - 🐦 Island Scrub-Jay
  - 🐦 Bahama Swallow
  - 🐦 Iceland Gull

Let me start by saying that some of these regional names are bogus. I have it on good authority that Philadelphia Vireos, Nashville Warblers, and Atlanta Falcons have very extensive ranges that may or may not include the cities of their names, and Orchard Orioles are sometimes seen outside of orchards. As you can see, this classification system still has a few bugs to work out, but the fact remains that somebody named these birds on the basis of where they were seen.

However, regional descriptors are very important. The bird commonly called the robin in this country is actually named the American Robin, and it is a different species from the

> ### *Fun Fact*
> The Prairie Warbler does not live on the prairies, but it does spend its winters in grassy woodland clearings known locally in the south as "prairies"
> *(The Birder's Handbook)*

robin found in Europe. But just to keep you on your toes, we do have an infestation of *European* Starlings in this country, which stemmed from a release of just 60 of these birds in New York's Central Park in 1890 – a population that grew and spread to the Pacific coast in just 60 years.

You will note that the regional part of the names can range from very general to quite specific. It can describe a hemisphere (north/south or west/east), as in the first two examples, or a relatively small island. The Island Scrub-Jay is a favorite of mine, because it's a bird that I have seen and my older and more bird-wise brother has not. He got involved in this addictive habit more than twenty years before he dragged me into it, but has never been to the only place these birds are found, Santa Cruz Island in the Channel Island chain off California. It looks much like the Western Scrub-Jay, but is larger.

Having a bird named after a state can be misleading. The ranges of the Florida Scrub Jay, the California Quail, California Gull, and Virginia Rail cover a wide area. The Connecticut and Tennessee Warblers only pass through those states during migration. And the bird that many call the Oregon Junco, actually a subspecies of the Dark-eyed Junco, can be seen throughout the west.

5. Unpronounceable names
   🐦 Prothonotary Warbler
   🐦 Garganey
   🐦 Chachalaca
   🐦 Cordilleran Flycatcher
   🐦 Guillemot
   🐦 Lazuli Bunting
   🐦 Common Pauraque

These names, while strictly not unpronounceable, are subject to mispronunciation and to controversy about proper pronunciation. Do you suppose their only purpose is to separate novice birders from the seasoned experts?

6. Names that are just plain wrong
   🐦 Pelagic Cormorant
   🐦 Black Oystercatcher
   🐦 Calliope Hummingbird
   🐦 American Redstart
   🐦 Juncos

For those of you who live more than a few hundred miles from a coastline, pelagic is defined as, "of the ocean surface, or open sea, especially as distinguished from coastal waters." Pelagic birds, then, are those that spend most of their lives on (or over) the bounding main. Think albatross, a bird that soars for miles over oceans without ever flapping its wings. Near the opposite end of the pelagic bird spectrum are the tiny Red and Red-necked Phalaropes, smaller than an American Robin, who nonetheless make a living out on the open ocean, picking plankton off the surface. They also do that on inland waters on their way to and from their arctic breeding grounds, but most of their life is spent at sea. The so-called Pelagic Cormorant is firmly rooted to shore, and the aforementioned *Dictionary of American Bird Names* says it is no more pelagic than any other cormorant.

Someone hearing the name "oystercatcher" might reasonably assume that oysters might do something that would require a chase before they could be "caught." However, oysters are not particularly known for their speed. It is a mystery why any bird would have a name suggesting that it was any kind of accomplishment to catch one. The American Oystercatcher does feed on oysters, but it prefers the couch-potato type oyster rather than the more athletic type. According to *The Birder's Handbook*, these birds either sneak up on open oysters and plunge their bills between the shells to sever the adductor muscle before the bivalve can close, or they hammer away at the shell to break it open. So, yes, they are working for their supper, but catching it, no. Their West Coast cousins, the Black Oystercatchers, have it easier – they pry limpets off of intertidal rocks. Limpets, being mollusks, aren't going to set any speed records either. (Think snail.) The more adventurous Black Oystercatchers also feed on mussels, which are not as tough as oysters to get into.

The name Calliope Hummingbird conjures up the image of a big, noisy steam-driven musical instrument. Calliope was the Muse of epic poetry, which in Greek means "beautifully voiced." And yet it is the smallest of our hummingbirds and notable for being one of the quietest. Go figure!

If you hear that there is an American Redstart in the neighborhood and want to go looking for it, you would be well advised to check out your field guide. This bird has no red on it – from start to finish.

The name Junco comes from the Latin for rush, or reed, suggesting that they hang out in wetlands. Nope.

7. Names that seem wrong but are really accurate
- Ruby-crowned Kinglet
- Golden-crowned Kinglet
- Kingbirds
- Ovenbird

Most of the time, the kinglets are pretty plain little birds, and you might wonder where anybody got the idea that they are crowned. But when they start to get excited, they show a little patch of red or yellow on the top of the head. For example, they consider pishing (discussed in chapter seven) to be the avian world's version of telemarketing, and it makes them angry. When a Ruby-crowned Kinglet gets really juiced, it can look like the top of his head is on fire. Quite a sight!

Kingbirds, like kinglets, are not terribly impressive or regal in appearance, but they are deemed to have earned that name because of their aggressive, dominating nature. But don't use that explanation when talking with any kings you happen to know.

Ovenbirds are not known to hang out in bakeries, nor are they known for being a great pie filling (unlike those 4 and 20 blackbirds). But their nest, built on the forest floor, resembles a small dome-shaped oven.

8. Names aggrandizing someone
- Brewer's Blackbird
- MacGillivray's Warbler
- Cassin's Auklet
- Dryden's Plover[3]

---

3. Not yet in production, but coming to a wetland near you after this book reaches the *New York Times* best seller list.

Talk about immortality! Name a bird after someone and people will talk about him or her forever. Not surprisingly, this is a very large class of bird names. Until this writing, I was under the impression that people named birds after themselves, but most are named for noted ornithologists or people who gained their fame in lesser fields. Many of the names were bestowed by John James Audubon himself.

9. Names with fascinating derivations
- Booby: When discovered by seamen on isolated islands, these birds had no concept that humans could be a threat to their safety. So they made no attempt to get away or otherwise defend themselves. So they were given a name that means "stupid." Disappointed?
- Bufflehead: I always thought that Bufflehead was a bit of a slur, a name one child might call another in anger or disdain. But actually, the name comes from someone's impression that this duck has a head shaped like that of a buffalo (actually, bison). If you see that resemblance too, perhaps you should be writing this book. For me a more apt name would be the one my neighbor gives them, Highway Patrol Ducks. (Most California Highway Patrol cars are black and white.)
- Aplomado Falcon: "Plumbum" is the Latin word for lead, which has been used as the weight at the bottom of a plumb-bob, used by craftspersons to determine exact vertical. The "stoop," or dive after prey, of this falcon is nearly straight down, and the Spanish verb for "to plumb" is aplomar.
- Gull: Celtic, Cornish, and Welsh languages, along with Latin, have various words that mean "throat," and they sound somewhat like "gull." It is presumed that the name comes from the birds' willingness to swallow anything, often whole. If you see a gull trying to swallow a starfish, it isn't a pretty sight.

- Nuthatch: This name comes from the birds' tactic of wedging nuts into crevices and hacking them into small pieces. Why aren't they called nuthacks? Because the experts said so, that's why.
- Plover: After the Latin word for rain. Several explanations try to rationalize the relationship of these birds to rain, but none of them holds water (pun intended). According to the *Dictionary of American Bird Names*: "There seems to be no justification or known valid reason for the name."

10. The rest of the names
This category includes all of the names that don't fit into one of the above. This category makes the *Birding Lite* System of Classification complete.

"The very idea of a bird is a symbol and a suggestion to the poet. A bird seems to be at the top of the scale, so vehement and intense his life. . . . The beautiful vagabonds, endowed with every grace, masters of all climes, and knowing no bounds -- how many human aspirations are realised in their free, holiday-lives -- and how many suggestions to the poet in their flight and song!"

...John Burroughs

chapter five

Look It Up
Essential References for Birders

A birder's field guide is much like a dictionary – It is easy to find the bird you are trying to identify, if you know its name!

The field guide is one of two fundamental needs of birders – the other being a decent pair of binoculars. This book is your basic reference source for identifying the birds you see and hear in the field. It is called a "field" guide because it is intended for taking out into the field with you when you are birding, not because it will guide you through the field. For that, you are on your own. But while some of them will fit in the patch pocket of your cargo pants, others require some sort of holster, shoulder bag, or backpack for easy toting. Some birders carry an abridged version in the field and have a more complete reference book for looking it up at home or in the car. There is no "right" way.

Which Field Guide Do I Need?

In chapter one you were cautioned not to call a field guide a "bird book," lest you garner the disdain of your fellow birders. Open hostility is unlikely, but why take chances? In this chapter we will define what makes a book about birds qualify as a field guide. This is not to say that other books are not useful additions to your battle gear, but you definitely need a fully quali-fied field guide.

If you shop around for a field guide, you will doubtless find that there is a wide variety of them, and each has its own following of knowledgeable birders who believe that it is the pick of the litter. But you will have to make a decision on which one to start with, unless you are filthy rich – then you will just have to decide which one will be your faithful companion. To assist you in this decision, we will describe the information you can expect to find in a trusty field guide and the variations on the theme. You may end up just buying the guide that a store clerk recommends, but at least I tried. (Sigh!)

If you have already completed the task I gave you in the previous paragraph, you may have discovered that field guides are arranged in a very peculiar way. There seems to be no rhyme or reason to the order in which the birds are shown. The arrangement certainly hasn't been designed to help you find the bird you just saw – it isn't by color, size, or any of the characteristics you first noticed when you saw the bird. It isn't even alphabetical. What's going on here?

Well, when you calm down, you will notice that, for the most part, similar birds – gulls, ducks, hawks, woodpeckers, hummingbirds, LBJ's, etc. – are clustered together in the guides. That's a help. Other than that, though, the order of these groups seems pretty random. However, all you need to know to quickly find the bird you are looking for is to remember the order in which the birds evolved. See? It's easy! The only trouble is that, with the advent of DNA analysis, the exalted leaders of bird-dom have decided that the order shown in my field guide, published in 2000, is wrong. So the guides published later have jiggered the order. My advice? Get over it! When you take over the world, you can change it.

There are some books, often calling themselves beginner's guides, which show the birds in logical order – by color, for example. But these books usually show a relatively small number of birds, and the descriptions are by no means as complete, so they don't qualify as field guides. They can be very helpful at first, but you don't want to relegate yourself to the permanent status of a beginner, do you? In any case, if you take one of these books out with you when around **real** birders, pay no never-mind to those smirks and snickers.

Back to choosing your field guide – your first task will be to determine what part of the world you want to have covered by your field guide. My primary reference is a North America guide, but there are guides for different regions of the continent, such as east or west. The advantage of the latter is that they are smaller and, containing fewer birds, are easier to use because there are fewer birds to choose from. One disadvantage is that eastern birds sometimes become vagrants in the west, and vice versa. Another is that your western guide won't be of much use if you go on a birding safari to the farthest reaches of the eastern seaboard.

Of course, if you are lucky enough to score a birding trip to Costa Rica or Kazakhstan you will need to get a field guide appropriate to those places.

Nearly all field guides contain the following information to help you identify birds:

1. The bird's common name and scientific name.
2. A picture or pictures of the bird. While some guides use photographs, the more useful ones (in my not-so-humble opinion) have realistic drawings of the bird in several plumages – juvenile and adult, male and female (if different), breeding and non-breeding, and in the air and on land (or in water).
3. The size of the bird, including wingspan for larger birds.
4. A map showing the range of the bird in summer, winter, and migration, and also areas where it can be found all year.
5. A written description of the bird in different plumages.

6. A written description of the sounds made by the bird.
7. A written description of the range, with details about habitats where it can be found.
8. A brief description of each family of birds, or in some cases, smaller groupings of like birds.

You should also look at the beginning section of each field guide you are considering, as it contains a wealth of information about birds and birding. Most field guides provide detailed drawings that identify the terms in common use in the guide and by birders to name parts of the face, wings, and other parts of the birds, including supercilium, eye ring, crest, wing bars, etc.

Some of the more popular field guides are listed in chapter ten. And don't forget – there is no law or birder code of ethics that restricts you to a single field guide. If you cannot find a picture in your main field guide that looks just like the bird you saw, another one might show a closer match.

To Carry or Not to Carry?

In my experience, it is not always necessary to carry a field guide. Perhaps it is useful to describe different types of birding ventures.

Birding for enjoyment:
One could argue that birding is always for enjoyment, but what I mean here is being out among the birds just to feed the soul and not for any of the other reasons discussed below. For example, when I am birding a familiar area where the bird population is fairly predictable, I don't really expect to see a bird I don't recognize. I am just out to "meet and greet" my avian friends, enjoy their beauty, listen to the music, and watch their antics with amusement. Some people may say this activity should be called "bird watching" (see chapter one), but that doesn't affect what I am doing, and the birds don't care either.

If I happen to see a bird I don't recognize or am not certain about, I can record the information to take home and confirm my tentative identification or, in rarer cases, identify a bird I don't recall seeing before. The recording can be mental, on paper, on my pocket voice recorder, or photographic. So my field guide generally stays at home.

Hot on the trail of a rare bird:
There is nothing like a hotline report of a rare vagrant bird to bring birders out of the woodwork. In these cases, I tend to be highly focused on that bird, particularly if it is a potential addition to my life list. Of course I want to be certain of my sighting, but I do that mainly through researching pictures, sounds, and habits of the bird before I go out. It is a good idea to have something to refer to in the field, and that can be either my field guide or material I have printed from the web.

Birding an unfamiliar area:
When I am away from home, I will at some point be looking specifically for birds to add to my life list, and the chances of seeing a bird that I do not recognize increases greatly. So my field guide is always with me. Even if I have researched several target birds for special attention, there is always the possibility of seeing a different new bird.

Leading bird walks for others:
See? I have great hopes for you – already assuming that you will become a mentor to other novice birders. If you are leading a bird walk, it will probably be in an area where you already know most of the birds. However, sometimes you will see a really cool bird off in the distance, beyond the range of good sighting with binoculars or even a spotting scope. Or perhaps it is in the underbrush and some members of the group get only fleeting looks at it. Or maybe you will be able to identify it by sound. In these circumstances it is great to have a field guide along to flip open and show a picture of the bird to the neophytes.

Organized bird counts:
When participating in a Christmas Bird Count or a local Birdathon, the count leaders can be sticklers for documenting the rarer birds that are reported. So unless you are an expert, it's a good idea to have your field guide with you.

The foregoing is moot if you have marched confidently into the 21st century and have one of those smarty-pants phones with a comprehensive bird identification "app" installed. Basically, it gives you a field guide and birding software in the palm of your hand. But I'm not jealous. Nope. No way. Uh-uh. Nothing but the printed page for me. But if this book sells....

Computer Software

You can also look it up on your computer. There are a number of computer applications that fall under the rubric of birding software. But I have found only one, *Thayer's Birding Software*, that provides the kind of information you would find in a field guide. It would be a stretch, however, to call it a "field guide," even though technically you could take it into the field on a laptop. I first ran across this software in the visitor's center of a wildlife refuge and had to have it!

This software provides most of the typical field guide information, such as name, picture(s), range map, habitat, and behavior. The pictures are high quality photographs, and often show several plumages, although not as many as most field guides. It also has several features that don't lend themselves to the printed page. For example, it contains the recorded sounds of birds, so you don't have to rely on those verbal descriptions that leave a lot to be desired. (Remember that silly quiz in chapter two?) It even has a little bird (Petey) that flies in and tells you how to pronounce the name of a bird. So if you have always wondered how to pronounce Pyrrhuloxia, Petey will help you out.

The software's "Identification Wizard" can help you narrow the possibilities if you have collected key information about a bird but still are unable to pin it down. Using selection menus for each characteristic, you can enter location (state/province), size (relative to other birds), habitat, color (either any color on a bird or a predominant color), field marks, and group. Field marks are limited to just four: crest/tuft, eye ring, wing bars, and white outer tail feathers. This feature will display a photo gallery of the birds that meet the criteria you have chosen, which can help you sort through the list of "hits." The gallery has links that let you zoom in on the photo, hear the bird's sound, or go to its full page "eField Guide."

Personally, I have not had a great deal of success finding the exact bird I am looking for in the Identification Wizard. I usually get a list that is very long and includes birds that are in no way similar to the bird I saw, or a short list that is clearly off base. In that case, I declare the discovery of a new species, the Dryden's Sparrow or Warbler or Gull or whatever. Unfortunately, I have not had much success (OK, none) in getting the powers-that-be to recognize these findings. But my failure to find the right bird with this tool may be because I have not fully utilized the options that allow refining the search. Or perhaps I have seen a bird in transitional plumage (juvenile to adult, breeding to non-breeding) that just doesn't look like any of the pictures in this tool.

 A really cool feature of the software, if you are into learning by studying and drilling (instead of my lazy-man's approach to just-go-have-fun-and-hope-something-sticks), is a large selection of quizzes that you can take. The quizzes are arranged in a variety of ways: some are for new birders, some are on a particular bird family, some are about the birds in a certain region, etc. Some quizzes show video instead of still photos. And they have sound! The great thing about these quizzes is that they are strictly on the honor system – nobody has to know how you did. If this is the way you like to learn about birds, this feature alone is worth the price of the product. It is great entertainment even if your mind is a sieve and your memory leaves a lot to be desired.

The Birder's Handbook is described below, but it is worth mentioning that *Thayer's Birding Software* includes the complete handbook as a reference. When you are looking at the "eField Guide" for a bird, you can jump to a page that describes the bird's life in lurid detail. If you have this software you may not need the book itself.

There are other types of applications that are also called birding software. As of this writing I have not found another that includes comprehensive field guide information. One is advertised to help you identify a bird based upon some of the same information used by the Identification Wizard described above. There are many that can serve as the place to keep your life list.

The Birder's Handbook

Most people, once they start paying attention to birds, cannot resist prying into their private lives. What do they eat? Where do they nest? How many eggs do they lay? How long does it take for the eggs to hatch? Who broods (sits on) the eggs? Who takes care of the chicks? What are the chicks like? And on and on. We think we can snoop into their innermost secrets just because they aren't human beings. Speciesism, that's what I call it!

Some people even have the audacity to want to know whether they breed for life or "sleep around." Can you imagine asking a person who is just a passing acquaintance a question like that? What gall! And why do you suppose we think that birds that mate for life are morally superior to the promiscuous ones?

If you just have to know that information, you can look it up in *The Birder's Handbook*. The cover of this book calls itself "A field guide to the natural history of North American birds, the essential companion to your identification guide." This tome has answers to the above questions – and more – on most North American birds. Birds that are not known to nest on this continent and those that have been recently introduced are not included.

For example, you can find the following facts in the "species treatment" for the Song Sparrow.

- They nest on the ground, in a cup-shaped nest built by the female.
- They typically lay and incubate 3-4 eggs at a time.
- The female broods the eggs, which hatch after 12-14 days.
- The chicks are "altricial" (immobile, downless, eyes closed, fed by parent – in other words, totally dependent).
- They fledge (fly) 9-12 days after hatching.
- The male helps out with caring for the young.
- These birds live mainly on insects, which they glean from foliage.

Wow! Now you probably know more about Song Sparrows than the birds do themselves!

In addition to the species treatments (described above), the book also contains dozens of essays on a wide variety of bird topics to answer just about any question you might want to ask. The book is printed with the species treatments on the left-hand pages and the essays on the right, and the essays are in proximity to the birds they cover. The essays are cross-referenced to the species treatments, so it is easy to tie the information together. *The Birder's Handbook* is not quite *essential* to your birding enjoyment, but close.

Resources for Bird Sounds

Suppose you hear a bird in the woods. You wait patiently for a good look at it, but the bird doesn't cooperate. It teases you with a few brief appearances, but you don't see it well enough to make a positive visual identification. Then it flies off and is gone. Birds can be so inconsiderate!

This frustrating scenario is one that is likely to play out many times before you get so proficient at bird identification that even a few brief glimpses are enough. So what can you do in a situation like this? Write it off as a mystery bird and forget about it?

You may have an option if you either have a "photographic" memory for sound, or carry a small recording device with you, as described in chapter one. If you can get a clean recording of its voice, you may be able to match the sound with recorded sounds. Getting a clean recording may be difficult for a couple of reasons. There may be other sounds in the environment – traffic noise, aircraft overhead, the rustling of the trees in the wind, or other birds. Or the frequency of the bird's song or call may not be in the range that your recording device can pick up accurately. These tiny devices don't exactly produce professional quality recordings.

But let's say you do get a clean recording. Then what? Hopefully, you have also made some notes about the bird's appearance. You will need this, because bird sounds are generally found through the names of the birds rather than through the characteristics of the sounds themselves. In other words, you have to listen to one recorded bird sound after another to find one that matches the one you recorded, and that can be very tedious. So it helps greatly to narrow the list of possible birds. There are lots of Little Brown Jobs out there, and you don't want to match your field recording to the recorded sound of all of them.

Recorded sounds can easily be found on *Thayer's Birding Software*, described above. The vast majority of its eField Guides have links to a sound recording, including virtually all of the songbirds. It doesn't have sounds of all of the albatrosses, but as you may have already learned, finding one of them in the woods is not generally expected.

You can also purchase a variety of audiotapes and compact disks that will entertain you with the sounds of birds. The audiotape products have the songs only of relatively common birds, but some compact disks contain over 500 bird songs. You can find these products online or in your favorite birdbrain store.

Finally, there are several web sites that contain bird songs for your listening pleasure, some also representing over 500 birds.

Local Resources

Let's say you see a bird for which you are pretty confident of your identification, and you have eliminated just about all of the birds that look something like it. But, being a relative neophyte in this business, you cannot say for sure. The range maps in your field guide(s) may not indicate that it frequents your area, at least not at the time of the year you saw it. There may be a local publication where you can look it up in order to gain confidence in your assessment. Conversely, it might convince you that you need to abandon all hope of sleeping at night if you record it in your life list.

In California's Monterey County, for example, we have one such resource, Don Roberson's *Monterey Birds*. The second edition of this book provides a detailed history of sightings of some 482 bird species in the county. Each bird account includes a graphic showing the likelihood of it being seen at different times of the year, and where in the county's diverse habitat the bird has been seen. It also provides information on birds that nest in this area. In addition to being a resource for local birders, it can be helpful to people who are planning a significant birding expedition to this rich birding area.

Roberson also collaborated in the publication of *Atlas of the Breeding Birds of Monterey County*, which is one of many regional breeding bird atlases in North America. There may be one for your state, if not for your local area. This can be another source for confirming your sighting, although birds that breed in the area where you saw the bird in question would probably show on the field guide's range maps.

So there you have it. There are quite a few resources to help you on your way to becoming a better birder. Chapter ten lists and describes additional resources to help you further expand your birding horizons. Some of those, however, are not as important as the ones described in this chapter.

A bird does not sing because it has an answer.
It sings because it has a song.

...*Chinese Proverb*

chapter six

Getting Up Close and Personal
Optics

*A walk without binoculars is like
apple pie without ice cream.*

It is entirely feasible – and perfectly acceptable – to enjoy the company of birds without artificially enhancing your visual prowess. You can have a jolly old time walking among them, watching them at your feeder or birdbath, and enjoying their antics and singing. But nobody will take you as a serious birder if you don't at least have a pair of binoculars – or, as they are often casually called, "glasses." Chapter one gave some advice on what to use as "starter" binoculars. But the fact that you have read this far might be the first sign of an impending addiction. If you didn't start with really good binoculars, this chapter provides additional information on how to choose them. This chapter also gives some hints on their use.

If you move on to purchasing a spotting scope, everyone will know that you are hooked. The upside is that carrying a scope gives instant recognition – perhaps undeserved – of your birding knowledge.

You can become a bird photographer at every level from simple snapshots to magazine-quality works of art. We will explore those options very briefly in this chapter.

All of the optical devices described here can enhance your birding enjoyment. But remember, you only *need* a good pair of binoculars. The others are just window-dressing.

Binoculars

By the Numbers

Size matters. Have you ever heard that before? Unfortunately, when it comes to binoculars it is all-too-commonly thought that size is **all** that matters. Let's say you are in the market for a good pair of binoculars after suffering far too long with grandpa's binoculars that he picked up at a war surplus store shortly after World War II, or the ones you got as a high school graduation present. Your birding buddy has a pair and seems pretty happy with them, so you ask to try them. Wow! What an improvement! The brand and size (e.g., 10x40) are imprinted right on the binoculars, so that's all you need to know – right?

Hold your horses, buster – it isn't that easy. If you purchase the exact model that your buddy has, you might be very happy with them. But if those binoculars happen to have the Swarovski name on them and you walk into a store with your credit card in hand, you might want to make sure that the store has a defibrillator on hand to restart your heart. You could say that they tend to be a bit pricey. Or if you buy a pair of 10x40's that fit too easily into your budget (a euphemism for cheap) you are likely to be disappointed by any number of their attributes.

So you might want to do a little more research to find a pair that fit both your needs and your pocketbook. If you find a store with a very generous loaner policy, you might be allowed to take several binoculars out into the field to compare. Good luck with that. You are more likely to find the perfect glasses if you bite the bullet and make the effort to understand what those size numbers mean, and what other specifications could help you make a decision.

Let's start with the numbers that all binoculars show (except the ones made up of two toilet-paper rolls taped together) – 8x32, 10x40, etc. The first number is the magnification, or power – the factor by which the binoculars enable you to see things as though they were closer. For example, 10x magnification let's you see things at 100 feet as they would be seen at 10 feet with the naked eye.

The second number is the size of the "objective" lens – the lens opposite the eyepiece – in millimeters. Other things being equal, with a larger objective more light enters the binoculars, thus the view is brighter. Birding is often done in low-light conditions. Can you imagine that some people often get up at the break of dawn to stalk birds? That is just not my style. But when tromping through the woods, even at midday, it is nice to have that extra light. So you want to lean toward a larger objective when selecting your binoculars. When I upgraded from some very old 10x40 binoculars to some 8x42 glasses, it was as though my subjects were suddenly illuminated. All other things are not necessarily equal, however.

It would be logical to assume that magnification is all-important, and that you should go for all the power you can get – if 10x is good, then 12x is even better. This is not necessarily so. There are two major reasons why you might do better with a more moderate power. One is that as power goes up, so also does the amount of shake that is inevitable with hand-held binoculars. That is why spotting scopes are almost always used with a tripod.

A more important consideration is field of view, or field of vision, a measure of the breadth of the image you are seeing. Think of the restriction of the width of view if you were to look for something through the cardboard center of a roll of toilet-paper. This is important in birding, because it can be difficult to spot a bird in your glasses that you have seen with your naked eyes. Because the little buggers often move around, a larger field of view affords you a better chance to keep a bird in your glasses as it flits from branch to branch. For the power-mad among you, here's some bad news – as the magnification goes up, the field of view goes down.

So the field of view is another important number for you to consider. It can either be expressed as a number of feet or as an angle in degrees. The former refers to the width of the field when focusing at a distance of 1000 feet. Think of a fence 1000 feet away and perpendicular to your line of sight – using binoculars with a field of view of 350 feet you would see 350 feet of the fence in the image. The other way of showing the field of view is just what you might think – the angle of view from the binoculars. An angle of 6.5 degrees translates to a field of view of 341 feet. You can do the math if you don't believe me. Some binoculars have the field of view imprinted on them; with others you have to look it up in the specifications.

It is a common misconception that the size of the objective lens is a good predictor of the field of view. I must admit that I was a proponent of that theory myself. But it is not true – 8x50 will give you a brighter image than 8x40, but the field of view may or may not be larger.

The binoculars' minimum focal length can be another important number to consider. Sometimes the bird you are trying to identify will be in shrubbery that is quite close to you. It may feel safe if you are very still, since it is in its element. As discussed in the Fun Fact later in this chapter, you can focus your binoculars at a specific distance into the shrub, essentially making the foliage closer to you quite transparent. Having binoculars that can focus down in the 5 to 10 foot range can be very handy.

Other Considerations
But enough with the numbers game. If you will pick up those old binoculars for a moment, you will notice that the eyepiece and objective lenses are not in

line. What's the deal with that? The reason is simple. Those binoculars have prisms cleverly installed at the corners so that the light reflects twice before it arrives at the eyepiece. These prisms are called "porro" (not porno) prisms. Without the reflections, those birds you are looking at would appear upside-down and backwards – and that just won't do, unless you happen to be looking at a bird like a bushtit that is actually hanging upside down.

But your birding buddy's fancy binoculars are just straight tubes with the lenses aligned. That must mean that they found a way to get around the upside-down and backward problem without prisms. Nope. The image needs to bounce around inside these binoculars too, and they have something called roof prisms. Now there's a really dumb name! Have you ever seen shingles on the top of binoculars? The name is rationalized by the lame explanation that the prism system is shaped *somewhat* like a pitched roof. Don't try to understand this – trust me.

So how do you know which kind to get? Generally, binoculars are less expensive to make with porro prisms. That means that you might be able to get porro prism binoculars at a lower price than roof prism binoculars of equal optical quality. However, the latter tend to be lighter and more rugged than the older design. In addition, roof prism binoculars can focus on birds at a much closer range than can those with porro prisms. That may not seem important to you now, but it can make a difference when you are trying to focus on the proverbial bird in a bush that is right in front of you.

Porro-prism binoculars

Roof-prism binoculars

When you consider the "cool" factor of roof-prism binoculars, the decision is a slam-dunk.

Here are a few other important considerations in choosing binoculars that you can live with happily ever after:

1. Coated lenses: The better binoculars have chemical coatings on the lenses to reduce reflections, thereby making the image brighter. But of course, the question is not just whether the lenses are coated or not. That would be too simple. There are different kinds of coatings, and binoculars have several lenses, each of which may or may not be coated. "Fully coated" sounds good, but only the inexpensive binoculars have that. "Multi-coated" means that the lenses have multiple layers of coating, and this is better than a single layer. But then some binoculars don't have all lenses multi-coated, and le crème de le crème of binoculars are "fully multi-coated." Try to keep that all straight when a binocular salesman is touting the virtues of a particular pair of binoculars!

2. Weight: Except for those old 16x war surplus binoculars, most binoculars don't weigh that much. But when you are into some serious birding, even small differences in weight can make a difference in how long you can hold them up to your eyes. If you are a 97-pound weakling like me, you might do well to go for smaller, lighter binoculars. Weight can also make a difference if you use the strap that comes with most binoculars to carry them around your neck. I highly recommend that you purchase a binocular harness (variously called binocular suspenders, neck-relief binocular strap, binocular caddy, binocular packstrap, or some combination of these terms) that puts the weight on your shoulders instead of the back of your neck. I can walk for hours with my binoculars suspended this way. You can get one at

outdoor gear stores, camera shops, or on the web. Better, yet, get it at a wild bird emporium.

3. Resistance to water: You may think you will be a fair-weather birder, but just you wait! When on the path of an elusive rare bird, birders will put postal deliverers to shame with the kind of weather they will endure. You don't want to take a chance of rain getting inside your binoculars and having them fog up. Don't settle for water-resistant or rain-proof. You want the gold standard – water-proof. Get binoculars that are guaranteed to be waterproof and fog-proof – they are filled with nitrogen to protect against fogging on cold days. Allegedly, I can drop my binoculars over the side of a boat, and they will float.

4. Armoring: This term is a bit silly. No, birds are not armed with tiny rocket-propelled grenades to defend their privacy. Armoring merely refers to a rubber or synthetic soft covering over the housing to make the binoculars more comfortable to hold and to provide a bit of shock protection.

5. Focusing controls: Most binoculars have a center wheel to focus both barrels at the same time. Since many people have different acuity in each eye, some binoculars have separate focusing on each eyepiece. But the center-focusing binoculars have a "diopter adjustment" on one side to correct for the differences, and this is sufficient for the vast majority of people.

> ## Fun Fact
>
> Did you know that binoculars give you x-ray vision? Well, that's not exactly true, but they do help you look into dense shrubbery to gaze upon a bird. That is because their shallow "depth of field," particularly at short range, allows you to focus at a distance that is several feet beyond the nearest part of the plant. This effectively blurs out closer branches to near invisibility. Try it!

Center-focusing is a great deal easier when you are constantly refocusing to different distances, something you will do when birding. Stay away from individual-eyepiece focusing unless you really need it – but now you know it is available if needed. An alternative if one eye is significantly better than the other is to purchase a monocular – why pay for two "oculars " if you can only use one? Finally, it is possible to buy fixed-focus binoculars, but don't even think about it – they are only good (but not very) for relatively long distances.

6. Adjustable eyepiece cups: Binoculars work best when your eyes are a certain distance from the eyepiece. Wearing glasses moves your eye farther away than the optimum distance. So most binoculars have adjustable eyepiece "cups" to allow for use with and without glasses. Older binoculars have a flexible rubber cup that you can fold back against the eyepiece when you are using glasses and fold up when not. Most modern binoculars have solid collars you either pull/push, or twist up and down, and they are easier to use.

7. Image stabilization: If you plan to do a lot of birding during an earthquake, you will definitely want this feature, which uses either electronic or mechanical gizmos (technical term) to steady the image even when the binoculars are shaking. You might also find this feature useful when birding on a windy day, looking at a bird at great distance, and after a long day of holding binoculars up to your eyes. People who have image stabilization love it, but it's natural to have a certain amount of loyalty to something for which you have paid a princely sum. Of course, the converse is also true – people like yours truly who do not have binoculars with this feature smugly bask in their savings because they are firmly convinced that they don't need it.

Telescopes

Binoculars bring the little birdies much closer to you, visibility-wise, so that you have a better chance of appreciating them in all their beauty and identifying their species. Telescopes, more commonly referred to by birders as "spotting scopes," can bring them significantly closer. Although you don't *need* a spotting scope to be a card-carrying birder (or bird watcher, if you prefer), you might find that you really *want* one. So dog-ear this page now, for future reference. While this section probably doesn't tell you everything you need to know to select a spotting scope, it is a place to start your quest.

Most of us first heard of telescopes as a tool in the study of astronomy. There are several significant ways in which birders' spotting scopes differ from the devices used for stargazing.

1. The most obvious difference is in size – and we aren't just referring to the telescopes you see in observatories. Even most personal-use astronomical telescopes have a very long barrel, whereas spotting scopes are quite compact. This makes them more practical for carting around in the field.

2. As with binoculars, telescopes and spotting scopes have an inverse relationship between power and field of view. Most astronomical telescopes have greater power and narrower field of view than a practicable spotting scope. You cannot really use the power of an astronomical telescope for spying on birds due to ground effects that come into play in birding. Heat waves rising from the earth, dust, fog, smog, glare, and air currents during the day all conspire to reduce your viewing pleasure, and these effects increase with the distance between you and the bird. So while you could bring a far-away bird much, much closer with a 200x telescope than a 20x spotting scope, the image can be so blurry that you really haven't gained anything.

Most spotting scopes don't offer more than 60x magnification.

3. Spotting scopes also give you an upright image of your subject, which is much more important in birding than in stargazing. If you were paying attention in the section above on binoculars, you can probably guess that spotting scopes contain prisms instead of just lenses and magnifying mirrors. Just as in binoculars, spotting scopes can have either porro prisms or roof prisms.

4. Finally, spotting scopes tend to be more rugged than astronomical telescopes. That is important so that they will survive being carted around in the trunk of your car. (News Flash: Some of the primo birding spots involve driving over less-than-ideal roads.) And carrying a spotting scope around in the field also subjects it to many opportunities to be jarred or, heaven forbid, dropped.

Selecting One

When selecting a spotting scope you will be faced with many of the same questions as in selecting binoculars – power, size of the objective lens, field of view, lens coatings, armoring, waterproofing, and weight. Most spotting scopes have variable eyepiece lenses so you can zoom in on your subject – usually by a factor of three. Powers of 15-45x and 20-60x are pretty typical.

One optional feature that you don't find on binoculars is an angled eyepiece. The eyepiece is set at an angle of 45 degrees above the axis of the barrel. Some people (including yours truly) prefer this style because it lends itself to more comfortable viewing. An advantage of the straight spotting scope is that you can place the scope at a slightly

Scope with angled eyepiece

higher elevation when you are viewing from a place that has tall vegetation between you and the birds you want to see.

 One nice variation on the angled-eyepiece spotting scope is a mounting system that allows you to rotate the body of the scope along its axis. This can be particularly handy when you are sharing your scope with others. Don't let this get out, but I confess that I sometimes use a spotting scope to look at animals other than birds. For example, in my volunteer work at Point Lobos State Reserve, visitors really enjoy seeing sea otters up close and personal. I am tall, and some visitors are vertically challenged. So after zeroing in on an animal with the eyepiece above the barrel, I can rotate the scope so that the eyepiece is to the side or even below the axis, making it accessible to someone quite a bit shorter. Carefully done, this is much less likely to change the aim of the scope than would jacking the tripod up and down.

Scope with eyepiece rotated to side

Then there is the little matter of the optical quality of the lenses. This can be difficult for you to judge by yourself. A two thousand dollar scope will probably have better lenses than one that costs "only" five hundred dollars. This isn't necessarily so, but is not a bad assumption. Only you can judge what quality you need. The best way to determine that is to compare them side-by-side under identical conditions and see if you can tell the difference in the sharpness of the image. You may get some help by searching for telescope reviews online and by talking with scope owners. In any case, you are less likely to be disappointed if you stick with a quality brand name.

Holding It Up

Did someone mention a tripod? How handy – I was just getting to that! If you decide to purchase a spotting scope, you will also need a sturdy tripod. That old one you have kicking around in the attic may or may not fit the bill. Cameras and spotting scopes use the same thread size for attaching to the pan head, so your camera tripod will probably hold your scope. The operative word, however, is sturdy, not because the scope is heavy but because you just might encounter wind at times. And it is mighty difficult to get a good look at a bird at one hundred yards or more if the scope is bouncing around in the wind.

While a tripod is a tripod is a tripod, there are several considerations in selecting one, and you would do well to look carefully before buying. If possible, try several designs before deciding. While it might be difficult to find a store that will allow you to take them out on loan, if you know several birders you can offer to carry and set up the scope at times.

1. Weight is a factor that most people need to consider. Remember – you might be walking several miles in your quest for the perfect bird, and you don't want a scope/tripod rig that will discourage you from carrying it. Some have said that a lightweight tripod is a flimsy tripod, but like the song says, "It ain't necessarily so." My lightweight tripod (I used one just like

Tripod "stretcher' and lever-type leg-locks

it before purchase, by the way.) has stiffeners that form a triangular crosspiece, or "stretcher" that connects the bottom of each upper section of the legs. I gladly trade a little bit of stability for the ease of carrying. But you do want to satisfy yourself that the tripod you purchase will be sturdy enough to be reasonably stable in the wind and to stand up to the abuse you will give it.

2. Also try the locks that secure the telescoping legs in position. Do they securely lock the sections in place, or is there a tendency to slip? And how easy is it to operate them? You may often find that there is no level place to set your tripod, necessitating changing the length of one leg – a trial-and-error process. Tripods have traditionally had collars that you screw down to tighten, while some newer models have levers that you flip down against the leg to tighten and flip out to allow the section to slide. You can see the lever type in the photo of the tripod stretcher.

3. The pan head is the gizmo at the top of the tripod to which you attach the spotting scope. It gives you the ability to "pan" the scope (move it from side to side) and tilt it up and down. Tripods generally come equipped with a pan head, but it is also possible to select the two pieces separately. Some photographic pan heads also allow tilting to the side to change your camera from landscape to portrait orientation. That is generally not necessary for use with a

Pan head. (Note three locking knobs, crank for raising, and quick-connect scope fitting.)

scope. One useful feature of some pan heads is a quick-connect fitting for your scope – an adapter that attaches to your scope and fits into a holder on the pan head. That can be handy if you separate your scope from its tripod frequently to transport it. A pan head is definitely something you want to get your hands on before purchasing. Thomas Jefferson *never* would have said, "All pan heads are created equal." The controls for changing the resistance to pan and tilt seem to be different on every pan head ever invented. Look for controls that are intuitive for **you** and easy to adjust to the right resistance.

A Few Tips on Use

Using a spotting scope isn't rocket science. You look through the small end and point the big end toward the bird. But it is not as easy as it sounds. Scopes have a narrower field of view than binoculars. (Think of looking for the bird through a paper-towel roll rather than a shorter toilet-paper roll – the longer barrel further restricts the field of view.) This makes it more difficult to view the bird in your scope, particularly if the bird is moving.

In terms of just getting your sights on a bird, it is easiest to spot one with the naked eye, binoculars are next, and a spotting scope is most difficult. Go figure! If the bird is stationary, it is helpful to note the vegetation or other objects close to it before graduating to binoculars or scope. You can often go directly to the scope after you have spotted it, particularly if the bird is far away. But sometimes it's better to take it one step at a time – from naked eye to binoculars to scope. This is particularly true if there are no notable benchmarks to lock in on, such as when you are looking at a bird on open water. Sometimes you will need to go back-and-forth several times between binoculars and scope before finding it in the scope. Don't blame me – I'm just the messenger here.

A bird in flight is nearly impossible to capture and follow with a scope unless it is very far away, is hovering (flapping its wings to hold a stationary position), or is kiting ("hanging in air"). I once trained my scope on a kiting Red-tailed Hawk and allowed several others to view it before it left the field of view. But that was a rare treat. Don't even try with a close fly-by – locking in on it with binoculars can be hard enough, and it takes practice.

Spotting scopes are most useful in wide-open spaces like shorelines, wetlands, and prairies. There are some birding sites where a spotting scope is not likely to do you any good at all. For example, when birding in woods, the birds are popping around among trees so much that it can be difficult to capture them even with binoculars. The rare exception (at least in my area) is if you expect to see an owl, which can remain perched in one place for a very long time.

Cameras

This will be a very short section, for the simple reason that I am totally unqualified to advise you on photographic equipment. My major claim to fame in the photography department is my failure to make sure the film was feeding onto the take-up reel when I loaded the film for my son's high school graduation. Talk about being in trouble! But perhaps you will find some nuggets embedded in the material below.

The gold standard of bird photography is the single-lens reflex camera with telephoto lens. If you are interested in taking magazine-quality photos, this is the equipment you will need. You are on your own here. Well, not really – there are plenty of resources to help you select equipment to suit your needs, but you will get no help here to find those resources.

There are other ways to get some decent bird photos to enjoy yourself and share with family and friends.

Digital cameras now come with prodigious zoom lenses and megapixels galore that, with a bit of luck, will enable you to do yourself proud in the bird photography department. However, since you will probably be purchasing a camera for a great variety of uses, your needs for information and guidance exceed my knowledge and ability to provide it here.

At last! We have finally come to a subject that I know a little about, digiscoping. This is a term invented a few years ago after someone figured out that you could get a pretty good image by coupling a digital camera with a spotting scope. Nearly all scope manufacturers will be happy to sell you an adapter that will help you orient the camera in the perfect position relative to the scope eyepiece. These adapters can be quite pricey – I believe they were asking about $170.00 for the one for my scope. Being pathologically cheap, I decided to see if I could take pictures without the adapter merely by placing the camera's lens up to the eyepiece of the scope. Lo and behold, I got a picture! But needing a way to center the camera lens with the eyepiece, I needed to fashion a ring that would fit snugly inside the rubber cup of the scope's eyepiece and accept the camera's lens housing. A PVC pipe coupling (cost: about a buck) did the job with just a little sawing and routing on my part. It isn't as elegant, easy to use, or reliable as an official-size-and-weight digiscoping adapter, but it works!

A few tips to increase your chances of success:

1. Zoom your camera's lens to a point where it no longer looks like you are taking the picture through a garden hose. This tunneling effect has been given the unlikely name "vignetting." I generally use maximum zoom (4x) on my camera, unless the image of the bird is then too big for the screen.

2. Set your camera for no flash. Many digital cameras have a significant delay when using the flash – between the time you push the button and the lens opens, and before it is ready for you to take another picture. The latter delay can last several seconds. This gives the bird too many opportunities to get on with its life before you get a good photo.

3. Set your scope to *minimum* magnification.

4. Click away like a madman – and delete the misses with impunity. This is particularly helpful when the bird is moving, eating, or preening.

There is a reason that they don't call this filmoscoping. You wouldn't want to try it with a film camera, because the success rate, particularly with the cheapo adapter, is not that high. And, of course, you wouldn't have the LCD screen on a film camera to help you aim and know when to click. Even with a digital camera, there are some mishaps with the lens alignment. The small, relatively dim LCD screen on my camera is very difficult to see in daylight, so I am often not sure the scope is even aimed at the bird – the inconsiderate beasties have this tendency to move, y'know. I estimate that some 90-95 percent of my photos go immediately to the recycle bin, if they even make the trip through the cable into the computer. But there have also been some gratifying successes, some of which have made great background on my computer desktop. You can view a few of these at *www.birdinglite.com.*

 Photos don't always have to be something you can show off, either. A merely adequate photo can be a part of your "field notes" that will enable you to identify – or confirm/prove the identity of – a bird in the safety and comfort of your home. Even if you aren't able to make the call yourself, you can email the photo to a more knowledgeable birder to help with the identification. There is more than one way to skin this cat!

If you plan to do some digiscoping you will want to select your equipment carefully. If you already own either a digital camera or a spotting scope, you will need to choose a compatible mate for it. Whether or not you plan to purchase an adapter, make sure all the pieces will work together. If you need to purchase a digital camera, get one with a large, bright screen and a lens that extends out from the camera's body when you turn it on. This facilitates centering the camera in the scope's eyepiece.

Digital camera binoculars provide another way to take photographs. They are basically a pair of binoculars with a digital camera integrated into it. Cheaper models have a separate lens for the camera, so the image is not magnified by the binoculars. But in the better ones the camera picks up its image from one side of the binoculars. So all you do is look at and focus on the object and press a button and, voilà! You have a photo – or even a video. Handy, no?

Handy, yes. But don't look for the best image quality, either with the binoculars or the camera. These units range in price from $60.00 to $200.00. You generally need to pay more than that just for binoculars to assure that you are getting good quality, and a good digital camera will cost at least as much as the combo. The camera may have up to five megapixels, but cheaper ones may have only 0.3 megapixels, which is fine if you like grainy pictures. When you consider that camera binoculars will give you 8-10x magnification, and you can purchase ultra-zoom digital cameras with equivalent magnification, you have to wonder what the advantage is of having a camera that is used like a pair of binoculars over one that is used like a camera.

One additional problem with the camera-binoculars is that the camera is mounted firmly between the barrels. This means that, unlike ordinary binoculars, with most camera binoculars you cannot adjust the spacing to fit the distance between your pupils. This may be a minor annoyance or a serious problem, depending on how much your interpupillary distance varies from the norm. This is a product you really need to try for yourself before you buy.

The value of this product to your birding enjoyment depends entirely upon how serious you are about birding. If it is something you enjoy doing at times when you happen to see a bird or you have nothing better to do, camera binoculars might work just fine for you. And it might be a nice gift for someone (for example, a child) who has recently become interested in birds – an interest that may or may not develop. But if you are becoming a serious birder you are better off with the optics described earlier in this chapter.

"Use what talents you possess: the woods would be very silent if no birds sang there except those that sang best."

...Henry Van Dyke

chapter seven

Heeere Birdy, Birdy, Birdy!
Attracting Birds

*Give a man a pish and he will think you
are a birdbrain. Teach a man to pish
and he will enjoy birds for a lifetime.*

Up to this point we have concentrated on your finding and stalking birds. How about getting the birds to come to you? This chapter describes strategies and tactics for doing that. However, it is necessary to point out that some bird lovers and bird experts frown upon some of the tactics. Also, the strategy of attracting birds is not quite as sedentary as it may sound. Proceed with caution.

Bird Calls

Bird calls include pishing, mimicking, and the use of recorded sounds. All of these techniques require you to go to where the birds are – even if that is just your back yard. They are used in an attempt to lure birds out to where you can see them and possibly identify them. They can be used when you are just looking for whatever birds are there, or when looking for a specific bird that has been reported in the area. And they can be used whether you have heard a bird or not.

Pishing

Pishing, or as some people call it, spishing, is the most commonly used technique to get a bird to show itself. Its name comes from the great tradition of onomatopoeia, or a word that sounds like itself (crash, boom, bang, zing, etc.) It is easy to pish (or spish) – just say it over and over. However, the idea is to make a sound that will attract birds, so you probably don't want to use your best basso profundo. In fact you don't "say" it at all – that is, your larynx is not involved, just the front of your mouth.

There are several versions of the pish. In fact, Pete Dunne has written a treatise on pishing, called *The Art of Pishing*, in which he posits why it works and describes a number of techniques. The book even comes with a CD so you can hear what all of his variations sound like.

Dunne defines pishing as an attempt to mimic the scolding calls of birds. His "surefire, patent pending" pish mimics the sound of a Tufted Titmouse in distress. The key to success, according to Dunne, is to sound excited, or better yet, **excited!** His rather anthropomorphic theory on why pishing works is that the birds are just curious. In other words they are just a bunch of nosy lookie-loos, just like drivers passing an accident on the road. But the book includes other sounds to accomplish this goal, such as those of the Eastern Screech Owl or other avian predator. Many birders would not include these sounds in the definition of pishing – if it doesn't sound like pish, it isn't pishing.

Without giving away the whole plot, there are a few of the book's suggestions that I like to keep in mind when I try to attract birds. Pishing is going to work better when I blend in with the surroundings (as in a wooded area) than when standing out in a field. I also try to think of other critters that might be in earshot, such as a cute little bear cub and its not-so-cute mother that may not be sympathetic to my goal of adding to my life list. I also try not to pish where normal people (non-birders) might hear me and report me to the authorities. And in deference to those who believe that pishing is a crime against nature, I eschew pishing in their presence.

To learn more, including "Ten Easy Pishes," you just have to get the book. And yes, Pete, I gladly accept kickbacks.

In my experience, I have had limited success with pishing. At times, it has had no effect at all. In some cases, it seemed to cause the bird to clam up – not exactly my aim. But the successes, when they happened, were quite entertaining. A few examples:

1. Pishing a Ruby-crowned Kinglet in coastal scrub treated me to my first sighting of the usually-hidden ruby crown.
2. Pishing in a stand of riparian willows resulted in my being surrounded by a dozen or more Chest-

nut-backed Chickadees, who seemed to be amused indeed by their decidedly non-avian visitor.

3. Pishing while sitting on my back deck once attracted a usually-raucous Western Scrub Jay, who then sat on the railing and made the softest, sweetest little murmuring sounds you can imagine.

4. Pishing up a Wilson's Warbler in willows brought him to a very visible place, from which he yapped at me for quite a long time.

5. If all else fails, frequently a Song Sparrow will suddenly appear and call, as if to say, "You called?"

In all of the above instances I was using the standard pish, learned not from the book but from other birders. Could it be that Dunne's standard pish doesn't work for me because the vast majority of my birding is done well outside the range of the Tufted Titmouse? Pishing has generally been most successful when it was done patiently, persistently, and while standing as motionless as possible.

One final caveat: Beware the wet pish. You might want to put a hand over your binoculars and not stand too close to the person in front of you.

Mimicking

Mimicking is where you follow Pete Dunne's advice to learn from the birds. This can be useful if you are an extremely talented whistler or have the capability to put your voice into ultra-falsetto. But let's face it, our larynxes are just too darned big to accurately mimic the warbles, tweets, cheeps, tzeets, and other musical (and non-musical) sounds of songbirds. While "chickadee" is an onomatopoeic name, our saying the name is not likely to impress the birds. We do better at the harsher sounds of birds such as California Quail. (Chicago! Chicago!) My best impersonation is of a California Sea Lion, which you won't find in most bird field guides. But it will not hurt for you to try... and try...and try – and you might hit pay dirt once in a while. Go for it if you have the talent.

Recorded Bird Sounds

Through the marvels of modern electronics, it is now possible to broadcast recorded sound at a decent level of fidelity with equipment you can easily carry out in the field. There are many compact disks that you can purchase, and if you have a portable CD player, you are in business. This technique, of course, is generally only useful when you are hot on the trail of a specific species. The birds will not be impressed by your attempt to entertain them with several hundred different bird sounds. However, if your CD player allows you to play a specific bird sound on demand, you just might be able to get that Rose-breasted Grosbeak you have been hearing to come a little closer if you play its song. Be sure that the CD you buy has the birds of your region, or the region that you will be visiting on your birding safari.

 There is another way to carry bird sounds out into the field. You can record them on the type of pocket recorder mentioned in chapter one. Although the fidelity of these devices may be significantly poorer than a CD player, you can record the songs or calls of just the birds you plan to stalk on a given trip. I have done that when traveling to an area that has different birds than my home turf – one bird song per channel on the recorder. The sounds are downloaded from my birding software or the web. I use these recordings mainly to help me identify the bird songs I hear or hope to hear, rather than to attract the birds. But it can be used for attracting them as well. My recorder records only through the microphone, which is fine for voice but not for music. If you can find one that allows you to hard-wire the sound from your computer, the quality is likely to be higher.

Other Enticements

Although birds are generally not interested in socializing with you, you can still lure birds to your yard by feeding them, "housing" them, or giving them a place to freshen up. The four main strategies are to provide bird feeders, bird baths, nesting boxes (or, as they are called by the uninitiated, bird houses), and the type of vegetation that provides them food, shelter or camouflage, or the opportunity to socialize with their own. You might want to keep in mind, however, that luring birds to gardens where house cats roam is not a great idea.

Bird Feeders
There are a great number of bird feeders on the market, and you can even build your own if you are handy at woodworking. They range from a simple dish, to the common hopper feeder that dispenses more seed as the birds eat the seed in the tray, to feeders that have elaborate mechanisms to discourage unwanted diners such as squirrels – no shoes, no shirt, no service. Although you can get them at hardware stores, craft fairs, and a multitude of other places, your best bet for finding a great selection and knowledgeable salespeople will be at a store that sells birdaphernalia such as a Wild Bird Center or Wild Birds Unlimited.

You never thought you wanted or needed to be a bird seed connoisseur, but it is good to pay attention to the seed you purchase for your feathered friends. While you can buy seed at grocery stores, you might want to be more discriminating. Seed you buy there may be old and dried out, and/or may not contain the most nourishing or appetizing seeds.

Different seeds attract different kinds of birds, so if there is a particular species you wish to attract – or

Above: *Basic Hopper Feeder*

Right: *"Squirrel-proof" tube feeder. Outer cage is spring-loaded to cover feeding holes when heavier animals land on it. (Chestnut-backed Chickadee)*

discourage – you need to know your seed. Make that last phrase your mantra. In addition, I'm sorry to have to break the news to you, but birds tend to be sloppy eaters. Quite a bit of the seed ends up on the ground beneath the feeder. This is good for the ground-feeding birds in your yard, but not so good if you don't like weeds. In the past, we roasted our seeds to sterilize them before putting them in the feeder. Believe me, the birds didn't mind. But then we discovered that Wild Bird Centers sell a Patio Mix of seed that will not germinate. Once again, it is a good idea to patronize a birdaphernalia store for good selection and good advice. They sell seed in bulk and in 25-pound bags, and that might also save you some money. You will be surprised how much you will shell out to feed your bird-watching habit.

Some people don't even want you to feed birds in your yard. Naturalists are generally opposed to feeding wild animals. This concern is mainly one of giving the animals human food that is not good for them (and maybe not for the humans, either!). If you feed, make sure you get them the good stuff – all the more reason to patronize a bird emporium. While there is some evidence that feeding wild birds can lead to harmful effects such as dependence upon feeders, on balance it appears to do more good than harm.

Nesting Boxes
I know! I know! *Everybody* calls them birdhouses, except those elite purists. But you are well into chapter seven now, and it's time to start acting like a birder. These edifices are not designed for long-term residence – it's just an indoor space (a **box**) to lay some eggs (in a **nest**) and raise the kids until they are ready to go off on their own. Not quite a rooms-by-the-hour motel, but close.

But these birdhouses (oops!) look adorable in your garden. And they often look like tiny houses, so call them what you want. But you have a decision to make – is it for you or for the birds? That is the distinguishing difference between a birdhouse and a nesting box. A birdhouse is designed primarily for you – a work of art in your garden. Some feel that there is an unwritten law requiring birdhouses to have a small peg just below the entry/exit hole. A nesting box can be (but doesn't need to be) quite plain, but **must not** have that peg. It is designed as a safe place for cavity nesters – parents and their chicks. These paranoid birds would not dare to raise their young in an open nest, and they see a peg as an invitation to a larger bird to perch and stick its head into the nest for nefarious purposes.

But the subtitle of this chapter is Attracting Birds, and if you install a nesting box where you can see it from

your house or a comfortable place to sit in your yard, the benefit is not all for the birds. You will see the parents-to-be arriving over and over with nesting material, then delivering food incessantly. As the time for fledging

> ### Fun Fact
> "Baby" birds are generally full size by the time they take first flight. And in many species they look very much like their parents at that time.

approaches, the parents' feeding effort will be supplemented by tiny pizza delivery helicopters – you won't want to miss this spectacle! If you are particularly observant you will get to see the little ones take first flight. After that, you will have the unique pleasure of removing the old nest and cleaning the poop out to make the box ready for the next family. It doesn't get any better than that!

If you want to buy a birdhouse, by all means go to a craft fair. But by now you can probably guess where I think the best places are to purchase nesting boxes. If not, it's time for you to review the previous section of this chapter. Same reasons. You might even find a cute one.

Birdbaths

There is nothing that tickles the funny bone of a bird lover quite like watching a bird intently take a bath in a puddle or birdbath. The water sprays everywhere and just rolls off the feathers. Part of the reason this is so amusing is that the whole process looks so haphazard. One has to wonder if the bath is really functional or just water play.

Birds may be messy eaters, but they are serious about personal hygiene. Many birds take "dirt baths," a practice more properly called "dusting." Water bathing is more common where water is readily available, but some birds actually follow a water bath with a dust bath, which lead some ornithologists to believe that it has some anti-parasitic function.

Since dirt is naturally available almost everywhere and water is not as plentiful, people often put out birdbaths in their yards. If you put it in a place where it can be readily seen from, say, your kitchen table, you can be entertained frequently. Some birds can splash away for several minutes (requiring you to refill the bath frequently), while others jump in and out several times. Modesty does not seem to play a role in bathing behavior. Birds will also come to your birdbath for a drink, giving you additional viewing opportunities. The birdbath in this photo sits on the deck right outside our kitchen window. (We have no cats.) The Oak Titmouse seems to be taking umbrage at sharing the bath with the House Finch (and the finch's buddy flying in).

Birdbaths can foul up pretty quickly, so you are in for a bit of work to keep it clean so diseases won't be spread among your avian buddies. Please do that for the birdies and also for yourself – a birdbath filled with clean water attracts more birds for you to enjoy.

Bird-Friendly Gardens
Birds will come to your garden if you provide for their basic necessities – food, shelter, water, and the opportunity to reproduce. Feeders, nesting boxes, and birdbaths provide a portion of the birds' needs, but they will attract more birds if located in a bird-friendly milieu. We warned at the outset of this chapter that the strategies for attracting birds are not entirely sedentary, unless you consider yard work sedentary.

There are numerous web sites you can easily find by searching for "bird friendly plants" or variations on that theme. Most of these sites offer general guidelines (rather than specific plants to plant), and the guidance excerpted below is generally consistent among the sites.

1. **Go Native!** The birds that reside in your area do so in part because the trees, shrubs, and grasses that grow there support them. Unless you live in an asphalt jungle, plants that naturally grow in the area provide most of the support. Then if your garden mimics the natural landscape, your yard will be a natural part of their habitat. Put another way, if you plant it, they will come.
2. **Diversify!** Different plants provide food in the form of nectar, fruit, seeds, or insects, and/or a place to hide from predators and/or a place to nest. Think "layers" – low shrubbery, taller bushes, and trees offer different opportunities for different birds. A variety of plants will provide a variety of benefits to a variety of birds.
3. **Be Prickly!** Shrubs with thorns or prickly leaves provide extra protection for birds, particularly when they are nesting. And many thorny plants, such as pyracantha, also provide berries for them to eat. But don't overdo it – at times you may want to tame these shrubs, and they have a way of fighting back.
4. **Be evergreen!** Conifers and other evergreens provide shade for birds in the summer and still provide cover in the winter when deciduous plants do not. You don't need mighty *Sequoia Sempirvirens*, as evergreens come in a variety of sizes and shapes.
5. **Provide an underground railroad!** Birds obviously are quite mobile and can quickly fly from one spot to another. But they may attract attention by doing so. This is good for you, the birder – but not necessarily good for the bird, which might be another animal's prey. Birds are attracted to areas where they can move furtively from one place to another. Plant groupings, interconnected with those in your neighbors' yards, are better than plants scattered hither and yon. Consider "natural fences" between yards.

6. **Be messy!** This is something you never heard from your mother, but you are hearing it from me. Immaculate manicured gardens are great for your social climbing, but they aren't the best for birds. Your feathered guests will prefer a little leaf litter here, a few dried seed heads there, a shrub left unpruned thither, and a pile of debris yon.
7. **Go light on the chemicals!** Use natural and organic fertilizers that will not harm birds. And if you must use pesticides, use them selectively and sparingly. Not only do you not want to poison the birds, killing off all the insects (most of which are not harmful to your plants) significantly reduces the food supply for birds.

There are a number of books that give specific advice on developing a bird-friendly garden. One web site, *www.yerbabuenanursery.com* provided by the Yerba Buena Nursery in Woodside, California, offers quite a bit of detailed guidance on specific plants. This guidance is summarized on the following pages with the permission of the nursery. If you go to the web site, click on Gardening Help, then scroll down to Bird-Friendly Plants for the Native Garden. Note, however, that most of the plants listed do very well in Northern California, but may not be suitable for your garden. Perhaps you can find a similarly-enlightened nursery owner who sells plants native to your area.

As much as I hate to end on a sour note, some birds, including crows and quail, can be quite destructive in gardens. They may eat your tender seedlings, expensive bedding plants, and the fruit from trees. Since this is a bird lover's book, we recommend non-lethal means of dissuading birds from their antisocial ways. Metal reflectors like strips of metallic Mylar or unwanted compact disks may scare them away for a while, but eventually the birds will learn to ignore them. Sunset Magazine's *Western Garden Book* recommends the use of plastic netting to block the birds' path to your vulnerable plants.

Yerba Buena Nursery
Bird-Friendly Plants for the Native Garden
(printed with permission)

Web site note: (* = best bird value for this resource)

Plants for Habitat: A wide variety of native plants provide nesting sites and protection from predators. Following are some of the most popular among the birds that frequent our garden.

Botanic Name	Common Name	Other Benefits
Arctostaphylos spp.	Manzanita	Nectar
Ceanothus spp.	Wild Lilac	Seeds, Insects
*Quercus spp.	Oaks	Seeds, Insects
Baccharis pilularis	Coyote Bush	Seeds, Insects
Myrica californica	Wax Myrtle	Fruit
Sambucus mexicana	Elderberry	Fruit, Insects
Rhamnus californica	Coffeeberry	Fruit, Insects
Heteromeles arbutifolia	Toyon	Fruit
*Salvia spp.	Sage	Nectar, Seeds, Insects
*Salix spp.	Willow	Insects
*Ribes spp.	Gooseberries	Nectar, Fruit

Plants for Nectar: Planted mostly for their value to hummingbirds, nectar-rich plants also attract a variety of insects, which are a food source for hummers as well as other species.

Botanic Name	Common Name	Season	Other Benefits
Arctostaphylos spp.	Manzanita	Winter	Habitat
*Ribes spp.	Currants and Gooseberries	Winter	Fruit
Salvia spp.	Sages	Spring-Summer	Habitat, Seeds, Insects
*Mimulus spp.	Monkeyflower	Spring-Fall	Insects
Lonicera spp.	Honeysuckle	Spring	Fruit
*Epilobium spp.	California Fuchsia	Summer-Fall	
*Penstemon spp.	Penstemon	Spring-Summer	

Plants for Fruit: Many species of birds depend on the fruit produced by these plants for the bulk of their diet. These shrubs attract an amazing number of birds in their fruiting season.

Botanic Name	Common Name	Season	Other Benefits
*Vitis californica	Wild Grape	Summer	Insects
Myrica californica	Wax Myrtle	Fall-Winter	Habitat
*Sambucus mexicana	Elderberry	Summer-Fall	Habitat, Insects
Rhamnus californica	Coffeeberry	Summer-Fall	Habitat, Insects
Ribes spp.	Currants and Gooseberries	Summer-Fall	Nectar, Habitat
*Heteromeles arbutifolia	Toyon	Fall-Winter	Habitat
Berberis spp.	Oregon Grape	Summer-Fall	

Plants for Seeds: The following plants produce an abundance of seeds which birds relish.

Botanic Name	Common Name	Other Benefits
*Ceanothus spp.	Wild Lilac	Habitat, Insects
Quercus spp.	Oaks	Habitat, Insects
Baccharis spp.	Coyote Bush	Habitat, Insects
*Salvia spp.	Sages	Nectar, Habitat, Insects
vvarious	Bunchgrasses	Insects

Insect-Attracting Plants: When we say "insect-attracting," this does not mean "pest-ridden." Most bugs are not garden pests, and many actually prey upon less desirable garden residents like aphids before being consumed in turn by birds. In addition to the particular plants listed here, plants which produce a flat-topped flower (i.e. Yarrow or Buckwheat) are excellent for attracting beneficial insects to your garden.

Botanic Name	Common Name	Other Benefits
*Quercus spp.	Oaks	Habitat, Seeds
Baccharis spp.	Coyote Bush	Habitat, Seeds
Sambucus mexicana	Elderberry	Habitat, Fruit
Rhamnus californica	Coffeeberry	Habitat, Fruit
Mimulus spp.	Monkeyflower	Nectar
*Ceanothus spp.	Wild Lilac	Habitat, Seeds
*Salix spp.	Willow	Habitat
Salvia spp.	Sages	Nectar, Seeds, Habitat

The Robin

The robin is the one
That interrupts the morn
With hurried, few, express reports
When March is scarcely on.

The robin is the one
That overflows the noon
With her cherubic quantity,
An April but begun.

The robin is the one
That speechless from her nest
Submits that home and certainty
And sanctity are best.

...Emily Dickinson

chapter eight

Seriously, Now!
Birding Obsession

We have Extreme sports, Extreme programming, Extreme Makeover, Extreme Ironing, even X-treme scooters. Are you ready for some X-treme birding?

There are many knowledgeable birders who do all their birding "in the moment." That is, they go out with their binoculars, perhaps also taking a field guide and/or spotting scope, happily identifying birds and occasionally seeing a bird that they don't recall seeing before. The remarkable thing about these birders is that, when they get home, they don't write anything down! In other words, they are not listers. There is absolutely nothing wrong with this behavior. If you fit that model, enjoy birds to your heart's content. However, I hope that you will be amused by just how far some people go in their quest for avian nirvana.

The rest of us need to have (or create) a challenge. And there are a number of types of challenges we can take on, depending upon whether we want to compete with others or just want to improve our own scorecard. If you suspect that this has something to do with left-brain dominance, you just might be right. Listing the birds we have seen is a very common way that birders "keep score" on how well they have done. You can improve your "score" by chasing the rarities. Or you can participate in "big" days, weeks, months, or years, which can either be a competitive or cooperative venture – or both. Yes, competitive birding does happen. And that is really X-treme.

Listing

Perhaps the one habit that distinguishes a birder from a bird watcher is the keeping of a life list, a list of all the bird species seen (and positively identified) within the birder's lifetime. In actuality, the list generally only contains the birds seen since the decision to start the life list, but why quibble over crumbs? The list grows rapidly at first, but the growth slows appreciably as the numbers swell. With over 800 species found in North America, there is almost unlimited potential for growth. So the birder's ego can swell as the numbers surpass the milestones – 100, 200, 300.... Naturally, in order to get into the multiples of one hundred, a birder must make quite an effort, and perhaps travel well beyond home base.

But how to keep track of this auspicious list? The proverbial back-of-the-envelope may suffice at first, but will soon become exhausted. There are several options, but the first decision you will make is whether to simply list the birds seen or to include additional information, such as the date, location, and other circumstances of the sighting. That decision will help you choose from among the following alternatives:

1. A simple ruled pad of paper or spiral-bound notebook will gladly accept practically unlimited numbers of entries. However, you might find that your chronological list doesn't give you a clear picture of your accomplishments.
2. Many birders start out by merely checking off the names in the index in their field guides. Very resourceful, and simple!
3. You can purchase a small checklist of North American birds, or many field guides provide a convenient checklist separate from the index.

4. The computer-minded birder might be more inclined to create the list as a word processor or spreadsheet file. This offers the option of sorting the information you have recorded in any way you wish – date of sighting, time of day, weather, phase of the moon, what you had for breakfast, etc.
5. There are a number of computer applications – stand alone or part of bird identification software, either to be installed on your computer or web based – that have already been designed for your life listing.
6. There are beautifully bound and illustrated books that you can proudly display on your coffee table or in your paneled library. You might even pass it on to your grandchildren when you go to that great Important Bird Area in the sky. I made the transition to obsessive birder after friends, who knew of my "fledgling" interest in birds, gifted me with one of the many such books, the *Audubon Life•List Journal*. It provides ample space for me to wax eloquent about the magical moment when I spotted and identified a new (for me) bird.

The bad news is that there are rules about what birds you can put on your life list. The good news is that you can make them up yourself, unless you are one of those birders you will read about near the end of this chapter. Some people will not list a bird until they have identified it by themselves. In other words, if they are with another birder who says, "There is a fill-in-bird-name-here," they won't put it on their life list until they see it another time and can name it by themselves. That is a warning signal of impending Birding Obsession, by the way.

Others will record a sighting identified by another birder, but only if they have seen it well enough to confirm in their own mind that, "Yes, that indeed is a fill-in-bird-name-here." Perhaps they will have a need to look it up in their field guide and compare a certain number of field marks before recording it.

On the lenient end of the spectrum, some listers will record a sighting even if they have just heard or caught a brief glimpse of a bird that is identified by another birder. For example, a Peregrine Falcon in full stoop flashes by in a nanosecond. The neophyte sees it, but does not get a good enough look to distinguish it from a) a hummingbird, b) a meteor, or c) a parachute-less sky diver. It matters not. If someone else says that it is a Peregrine, it will go on the list.

You get to choose where you want to be on this continuum. As you were undoubtedly told in your youth, "Let your conscience be your guide."

Some birders are not satisfied with a life list. They might keep an annual list and track how they do from year to year. Going a bit further, some make monthly lists, weekly lists, and even daily lists. If you start making hourly lists, the ghost of John James Audubon will appear in a dream to knock some sense into you.

Then there is the practice of making geographic lists. You can list the birds you have seen in your state, or your county, or your city, or your yard, or at your feeder. You can also make a list for each trip you take. The fun just goes on and on!

And listing birds sets you up for another obsessive behavior – setting goals! Where do you want your life list count to be at the end of the year? How many birds do you want to see in your county this month? How many birds do you hope to see on your fabulous vacation in Peoria? How many *new* birds?

If you enjoy listing but don't want to think of yourself as being obsessive, you can call your list an inventory. I keep a monthly list – no, inventory! – of the birds I see at Point Lobos State Reserve. It is an inventory, not a mere list, because I send it to others for their edification. That makes it research; *ergo*, I am not obsessive.

One final point on listing. If you are confident in your ability to identify some birds by sound, you are free to decide whether to include birds that you hear, but do not see, on your personal lists. If you are sharing your data with others, there needs to be some agreement with the recipients as to whether those observations are acceptable. For example, the person who keeps the Point Lobos master inventory has agreed to accept my aural observations. Some organizations that sponsor bird-counting events have their rules about heard-only birds. There may be some that even require the birds to be seen *and* heard, but I hope not.

Chasing the Rarities

If you list (or even if you don't), you may want to find out whenever a rare bird has been sighted, so you can go see it yourself. Many geographic areas have Audubon Society affiliates or other organizations or individuals that sponsor bird hotlines. The hotlines allow people to phone in and leave a brief message about birds they have spotted, and others to phone in and listen to the recorded messages. If you don't already know, find out if there is one in your area and program it into your speed dialer. (Warning: Obsession Alert!) One day, you might get to record your own sighting – a proud milestone indeed in your birding career.

Monterey County has a very active hotline called the "Bird Box," which many birders check religiously. Some go so far as to have a text message sent to their cell phones so they are able to find out right away when an unusual bird has been sighted. If a true rarity is proclaimed, one can often find a confluence of birders in the most unusual places.

For some people, however, it is not enough to chase just the rare bird reported in their area. Their antennae are continually tuned to reports of rare visitors from other continents. This is where it gets expensive! Say you live on the West Coast and hear that a Smew, a Eurasian species rarely seen in the Aleutians and "accidental" in the lower 48, has been sighted in Maine. What's a birder to do? You drop everything, jump on a plane, fly to Maine, hire a guide, and take whatever time it takes to find the bird – then fly home and resume your livelihood. Yes, it has actually been done!

Competitive Birding

Human beings are naturally competitive, so is it any wonder that they would make a contest out of birding? Here we are getting up into the very rarefied air of Birding Obsession. It isn't about the birds anymore – it's all about you!

All birding competition is not necessarily X-treme. The Christmas Bird Count (CBC) is not just a benign excuse to go out and get cold and/or wet – you are also competing for the honor of your birding community. The "competition" is friendly and often involves cooperation among nearby counties. And the emphasis is on fun and learning. But that doesn't stop some people from making grandiose claims, like calling their county the "birdiest" in the universe.

The Christmas Bird Count is an annual event, sponsored by the Audubon Society for over 100 years, in which "citizen scientists" compile a census of birds throughout the Americas. For more information, see *www.audubon.org/Bird/cbc/*. The book *Bird Brain-Teasers* defines the Christmas Bird Count this way: "*n.* A year-end migration of wooly-capped binocular users into wooded areas of the Western Hemisphere. One theory suggests it's a century-old ritual involving the counting of birds. A more plausible explanation is that the thick-soled species uses it as a method for burning off calories stored up from excessive winter feeding."

A "Birdathon" is another excuse to go out and count birds in a cooperative effort with other birders. Usually held in springtime and sponsored by local Audubon Society affiliates, it is a fund-raiser for the Audubon Society or some other worthwhile bird-friendly organization. In Monterey County, at least, it creates an inventory of bird species seen during a 24-hour period, rather than a count of each individual bird seen, as with the Christmas Bird Count.

The American Birding Association (ABA) publishes annual Big Day and life list reports. While not a competition *per se*, the scores are published in black and white with the highest numbers at the top. Now don't you want your score to be higher than that annoying pip-squeak you keep running into in the field? And don't you think that the scores are the subject of wagers that are made before the results are published? Of course there are rules, which can be found on the ABA's web site – and as you might expect, these rules bear little resemblance to what is written above about your own personal rules.

Birders who are itching for competition can establish any time period for their non-sanctioned contests. Big Week anyone? How about Big Month? Big Decade? Just win, baby!

Big [Period] events don't have to be competitive. Some birding festivals include a Big Day, in which participants fan out around an area to see how many birds they can see – just for fun. Big Years can be done for research purposes, too – to identify trends in bird populations, for example.

Building towards a crescendo of Birding Obsession, we have the story of a Big Year contest as told in Mark Obmascik's engaging book, *The Big Year: A Tale of Man, Nature, and Fowl Obsession*. This book chronicles the exploits of three contestants who competed to see who could produce the largest list of birds seen in North America in 1998. The men traveled some 275,000 miles as they crisscrossed the continent in search of common and rare species. They spared no expense and stopped at nothing in their vicious, cut-throat quest to outdo one another. It is an amazing and entertaining look into the minds of men who were truly obsessed.

But the pinnacle of Birding Obsession is clearly occupied by the Big Listers. Not content with a mere North American contest, these birders cover the globe in their list-making. Now we are talking real numbers. Instead of being confined to 800-900 North American birds and a few accidental visitors, they go to the ends of the earth to compile lists in the thousands. The current leader, the late Phoebe (actual name!) Snetsinger, used her considerable wealth to compile a list of 8,450 birds.

How many bird species are actually out there? Nobody really knows. Ms. Snetsinger's exploits are described in Dan Koeppel's *To See Every Bird on Earth*. However, the book is primarily about the manic journey of another obsessive birder, Koeppel's father, Richard. It is as much a tale of the father-son relationship as it is about Richard's lifelong obsession. At the time the book was written, there were 9,600 species *estimated* to exist worldwide.

What would make someone pursue this challenge? Phoebe Snetsinger is an extreme example of an X-treme group of people. She was an avid birder who, in 1981, was diagnosed with a deadly form of skin cancer and sentenced to "Three months of good health, then inevitable, rapid decline . . . and death within a year." She underwent basic treatment and then decided to make the most of her brief remaining days by indulging her passion for birding. Being the daughter of the advertising genius who created the Marlboro Man, she inherited a fortune that enabled her to do anything she wanted. The threat of going to unfamiliar, dangerous places meant nothing to her when she was living on borrowed time. Twenty years after the diagnosis, she died in a vehicle accident in Madagascar – on the same day she saw her 8,450th bird. (The above information is from Koeppel's book. Two books have been written about her exploits: her memoir *Birding on Borrowed Time*, published posthumously, and a biography, *Life List* by Olivia Gentile.)

Earth to Birder. . .

OK, now. Take a deep breath and settle slowly back down to earth. The foregoing is not a suggestion that your pursuit of birding pleasure will or should approach the intensity described in this chapter. Much of this activity, in fact, is the antithesis of *Birding Lite*. But I thought you would be amused to read just how far some people have taken this pastime.

I also encourage you to monitor your own engagement in birding, so that you don't find yourself sucked into the whirlpool of obsession. Consider the proficient skier who can continue to receive a recharge of endorphins year after year by skiing only the beginner slopes, or perhaps some of the easier intermediate slopes. Contrast this person with the equally-proficient skier who "needs" to blast down the advanced slopes, take jumps, and perhaps graduate to helicopter skiing. The steps between these extremes can be so deceptively incremental that one (either a skier or a birder) may not be aware of the progression toward obsession. Please remember: you get to decide how far you want to take this birding avocation.

"My favorite weather is bird-chirping weather."

... Loire Hartwould

chapter nine

The Tough Ones
Difficult Birds

*"It is not because birds are difficult that
we do not dare, it is because we do not
dare that they are difficult."*
(with apologies to Seneca)

Many birds are "difficult" in the behavioral sense.
Frankly, my dear, they don't give a damn whether
you identify them or not, and they aren't about to do
you any favors. They have things to do, places to go,
and birds to meet. And you are not on their agenda.
Your life list is of no consequence to them. As Walter
Cronkite used to say, "That's the way it is."

Birds are also inherently difficult to identify because
the little buggers keep changing. They may (or may
not) change appearance as they mature after leaving
the nest. The males may (or may not) look different
from the females. (This is called sexual dimorphism.
You can amaze your friends with your erudition by
laying that term on them!) And, of course they may
(or may not) look different during breeding season
from the rest of the year.

Birds may also have loose morals, anthropomorphic-
ally speaking. They don't always limit their urge to
reproduce to a mate of the same species. So we get
hybrids – not one species or another, but both. That
gull may be neither a Western nor a Glaucous-winged,
but a cross-breed. If you see a duck that doesn't re-
semble anything in your field guide, there is a good

chance that it is what my expert birder friend calls a "barnyard duck." These ducks tend to be common at urban duck ponds.

Bird Similarities

There is also a different kind of difficult – birds that look very much alike except for subtle differences. Here we may be talking about two very similar birds, such as:

1. Western and Clark's Grebes
2. Greater and Lesser Scaups
3. Long-billed and Short-billed Dowitchers
4. Allen's and Rufous Hummingbirds
5. Black-capped and Carolina Chickadees

Some of these pairs can be distinguished quite easily if one or two simple differences are pointed out to you. Other pairs can create arguments even between experts. Yet other pairs could be difficult were it not for the fact that their regions do not overlap. For example, the Oak Titmouse and Juniper Titmouse were once considered one species, the Plain Titmouse – a rather insulting name, don't you think? They look quite a bit alike, but all you need to do in order to distinguish between the two is to look for the "You are here" spot on a map. Finding a Juniper Titmouse would be a rare occurrence near the Pacific coast, or an Oak Titmouse east of the Sierra Nevada range.

There are other small groups of three or more birds that can pose a challenge, too. Subgroups of large bird families – for example, lighter-gray gulls, medium-sized terns, some sapsuckers, and the *Empidonax* genus of flycatchers (Willow Flycatcher and kin) can give even experienced birders fits. (You will learn soon enough which species are in this genus, and what makes it so tough. Don't fret your head about it now.)

One of the best sources to help you tease out the differences between these smaller groupings of similar birds is Kenn Kaufman's *Advanced Birding*, one of the Peterson Field Guide series. This book will help you with difficulties in identification, but many of the differences are so subtle, and the birds so determined to be difficult, that precise identification can be a formidable challenge. For example, when was the last time you have seen a hummingbird perch on a nearby branch, facing away from you, with its tail spread so that you could determine the exact shape of the tail feathers?

There are also whole groups or "families" of birds that cause birders of less-than-expert standing quite a bit of difficulty. Many birders take the easy way out and "not dare," as suggested in the paraphrased quote at the beginning of this chapter – pick off the easy or common members of the family and give up on the rest. But there is hope. Not hope in the sense that you will become proficient in identifying all these species by the time you have finished reading this chapter, but hope that you can have some semblance of a plan to become better at it than you are now.

Field guides often don't show the stage of maturity or seasonal molting of the bird you are seeing. For example, they may show juvenile and adult birds, but not "teenagers" – the juveniles that are in the process of molting to adult plumage. We all know that some human teenagers take great pains to disguise the fact that they are members of the human race. They don't want to look like their younger siblings, and they certainly don't want to look like their parents. Although birds don't seem to be as willful about it, they still don't fit the neat profiles you will find in your field guide. This is where a guide for a specific group can help, because it may have a photo or drawing that looks just like "your" bird.

A good example of this dilemma is a bird seen several times on a two-day trip to the Sierras, a region I had not spent a lot of time birding. This sparrow-like bird was quite plain, but had a yellow-green hint on the primary wing feathers[1] and also on the tail. There was nothing like it in my field guide. By luck, I had run across some local birders who asked if I had seen any Green-tailed Towhees, which they said were very common there. None of the birds I had seen had the patch of red on the head, as shown in the pictures of the adult Green-tailed Towhees. Nor did they look like the juvenile shown in my trusty field guide. As we were preparing to leave within the hour, I had no more time to look for one. After returning home I looked in a book lent to me by a friend (one of the sparrow books described in the section on sparrows later in this chapter) and found a photo of one of those "teen-agers" that looked exactly like the birds I had seen. Another lifer![2]

Over the years, I have seen numerous sparrows that didn't fit any of the pictures in any of my field guides. I was tempted to declare them to be a new species, Dryden's Sparrow, but thought better of it. So on a personal note, after ten years of serious birding I am finally figuring out the limitations of relying solely on field guides to identify every bird I see. Slow learner.

When you are ready to make the effort to get better at identifying certain kinds of birds, look into purchasing a guide to that group. Here is what it will offer:
- More complete descriptions of the characteristics of individual species of the group: size, vocalization, behavior, habitat, breeding behavior, etc.
- Some of the "family" guides offer more photos or drawings of plumages at different levels of maturity and different seasons, including what they look like in transition between plumages. You won't find the latter in most field guides.
- Guidance on things to look for to distinguish between similar-looking birds.

---

1. Primary wing feathers: the largest and outermost of the flight feathers. They appear at the bottom edge of the wing when the bird is perched.
2. Lifer: birder-talk for a new addition to one's life list.

❦ Detailed text descriptions of the individual parts of the birds' "landscape." These may describe a part of the bird that may not be shown clearly in your field guide, for example, a view from the rear or below. The typical profile view you get in your field guide doesn't help much if you are looking straight up into a tree. But the shape and color of the underside of the tail may be the clue you need to distinguish between two similar species.

Gulls

Gulls are difficult even though they are well-behaved, from the perspective of a birder. They don't flit about from branch to branch. So you will have no difficulty following them in the upper reaches of trees, as you will with the miscreants to follow. In fact, if you ever see a gull in a tree you probably will not confuse it with a warbler. All you have to do in order to get good looks at gulls is take a picnic to the beach and throw out a few chunks of bread. You will have no trouble studying gulls, and won't even need binoculars.

But gulls have other irritating habits that can make it difficult to identify any given bird. For one, they take up to four years to mature and not only have different plumage each year (or "cycle," as real birders call them) but also in between cycles. One gull book, the Peterson Reference Guide titled *Gulls of the Americas*, by Howell and Dunn, has 36 photos to cover all of the combinations from first cycle to adult of a Slaty-backed Gull.

Western Gulls (like all gulls) are brown in the first cycle. There is a difference among gulls as to the shade and the amount of mottling, and hotshots can identify the species in the first cycle. Since you are reading this book you are probably a novice, so don't even try to do that now. Late in the first cycle the Western Gull's head and breast whiten, but the rest of the bird is still brown. In the second cycle the back turns gray, but the wings are still brown. Gray creeps onto the wings in the third cycle, but there is still quite a bit of brown, particularly on the wing coverts[3] early in the molt. As adults they have gray wings with white edges. You see many more gulls in this stage than any other simply because once they

get their adult plumage they keep it for life. They continue to molt, but each succeeding set of feathers looks just like those of the year before.

Other parts of the Western and other gulls also change as they go through their several years of maturation. The tail and rump get progressively more white, and the bill goes from totally black to pale yellow with a decreasing amount of black near the tip. The characteristic orange spot on a bright yellow bill doesn't show up until adulthood.

Another disturbing habit is that gulls tend to be terribly conformist. Yes, there are differences in the shade of gray from one species to the next, but some of the differences are pretty subtle between one species and another. Throw in the vagaries of lighting, including your angle to the bird in relation to the sun, and you cannot rely too heavily on your sense of the shade of gray. Of course, the "masked" gulls (those with black heads, such as Franklin's, Laughing, Bonaparte's, Little, and – are you ready for this? – Black-headed Gulls) stand out from the rest, but even they tend to look a lot like one another. The Heermann's Gull is decent enough to follow the road-less-traveled, as they are easily distinguishable, with their unique plumage and bright orange bill.

---

3. Coverts: the shorter protective feathers on the front of the wings that cover the bases of the larger "flight feathers."

The clincher is that gulls aren't very choosy when it comes to selecting a mate, and it is not unusual for them to "cross the line" to mate with another species. And do you think a Western x Glaucous Wing Gull hybrid looks like either parent? Dream on! They may look more like Slaty-backed (dark gray) or Thayer's (light) Gulls. Or they may look like a different hybrid combination.

It is no wonder the authors of the Peterson gull guide call them an "equalizing force" among bird watchers, as an individual bird can humble even an experienced observer trying to come up with an identification. No single field mark will enable you to make the call – you need to look for a combination of marks. Specifically, plumage pattern, bill size, structure, head and neck streaking, eye color, leg color, and behavior all need to be taken into consideration.

If you see a gull you don't recognize, watch it long enough so that you can write down everything you see. Better yet, take a photo. Take several photos. Then repair to your study to compare your notes/photos with some authoritative gull guide such as the aforementioned. Just don't call it a Sea Gull.

Sparrows

"Sparrow" is a common classification of a large group of North American birds, not all of which have the word "sparrow" in the name. The group includes seedeaters, towhees, buntings, juncos, and longspurs, as well as sparrows – altogether some sixty-four species. Some members of this group, for example most towhees, juncos, and some longspurs, are distinctive enough so that they are not likely to be confused with mere sparrows, but it can still be quite difficult to "make the call" when you see a bird that belongs to this group.

There are two specialized guides written by James Rising and David Beadle that provide a great deal more information about sparrows than your field guide. They both provide the type of information described earlier in this chapter. The earlier book, *A Guide to the Identification and Natural History of the Sparrows of the United States and Canada*, has substantially more detailed descriptions of the natural history of the birds than the later book. It

is illustrated with excellent black and white drawings and color illustrations. The later book, *Sparrows of the United States and Canada: The Photographic Guide*, as its name implies, shows photographs of each sparrow in several different plumages. It is the latter that had a photograph that looked just like the Green-tailed Towhee "teenager" I saw in the Sierras.

In the Peterson Field Guide, *Advanced Birding*, Kenn Kaufman tells us that the common practice of identifying birds by field marks simply doesn't work so well with sparrows. These birds often don't stick around in plain view long enough for you to go through your mental checklist of things to look for. In addition, many *appear* to have a distinguishing field mark, like a central breast spot, but what you are seeing is caused by ruffling of the feathers that expose a darker color at their base.

Breast streaking is also quite unreliable as a field mark. Some plain-breasted sparrow species are streaked as juveniles. And feather wear[4] can lessen or essentially erase the streaking of sparrows that are shown as having streaked breasts in field guides.

---

4. New feathers, right after a bird molts, look crisp and fresh and may be edged in a contrasting color. As the months go by, feathers wear and lose this crisp look and edging.

What's a birder to do? Kaufman suggests a different approach, one in which you use the characteristic shape and behavior of the sparrow to narrow the choices. The method requires significant study and practice before you become proficient at it, but if it were easy, I couldn't include sparrows among The Tough Ones.

Warblers

This group of birds earns its place among The Tough Ones through a variety of attributes:

1. First of all, there are so darn many of them (over 50), and there are many similarities in appearance between species, especially among females.
2. Although there is a *relatively* large range in size (4 ¼ to 6 inches, excluding that monster, the Yellow-breasted Chat at 7 inches), they are basically tiny birds.
3. They are also very active, flitting about in dense foliage, often well over your head. In other words, they are "difficult" in the sense of the first paragraph of this chapter.
4. Most field guides do not do justice to the variety of plumages on display in this group of birds. If you really want to get serious about being able to identify them like a pro, you need a specialty book, such as the Peterson Field Guide called *Warblers*, by Dunn and Garrett.
5. Changes in warblers' appearance may be the result in feather wear as the time since the last molt gets longer, just as mentioned earlier in reference to sparrow breast streaking. So a bird seen in midwinter may look quite a bit different from the early fall pictures in your field guide. This phenomenon is enhanced among warblers due to the brightly contrasting plumage of this group of birds.
6. Oh! And one other thing. Most of them don't warble, or at least don't make a sound like anything I would call a warble. The plain old House Finch

would put most of them to shame with its warbling.

The book mentioned above gives you, in 650 pages, everything you need to know to become an expert warbler identifier, if you have the patience, fortitude, and photographic memory to overcome the difficulties listed above. The authors assure you that "... the identification of North American warblers is generally straightforward *given adequate views*." (Emphasis added – see item 3 above.)

The book points out that to identify the species of a particular warbler you are seeing, all you need to look for are:

- Wing bars and tail spots;
- Head patterns – e.g., crown stripes, supercilium, dark line through eye, eye-ring, and dark cheek patch;
- Whether the back is plain or spotted;
- A pale patch on the rump;
- Stripes or spots on the flanks or breast;
- Shape and size of the bill;
- Length of the tail;
- Extension of the primaries beyond the other flight feathers;
- Overall size;
- Vocalization;
- Behavior – e.g., posture, tail movements, foraging behavior.

See? There are only about twenty individual features you have to note as the bird flits about in the upper reaches of a tall tree. Note that the authors used the word "straightforward," not "easy."

But fear not. If you have the will, *Warblers* will show you the way by explaining a few key characteristics. For example:

1. If you study the taxonomy[5] of warblers, you can narrow the likely suspects for the bird you are watching by knowing which characteristics are more likely to be found in certain genera (plural of genus) of warblers. For example a sharply pointed bill may be a clue that the bird is in the genus *Vermivora.*
2. Foraging behavior is also a clue to the identity of a warbler, as each species has its own preferences. Some glean insects from leaves, some forage on the ground, some engage in "sallying" (commonly called "fly-catching"), and some dine on fruits and berries when they are available.
3. Other behaviors such as tail-bobbing, upright tail, tail-fanning and wing-spreading, and raised crown feathers may also narrow "your" warbler down to just a few. Take note if you see any of these actions, although they may or may not be mentioned in your field guide.

The Peterson Field Guide[6], *Warblers,* has many more drawings of warbler species than you will find in any true field guide, including both male and female, adult and juvenile, and spring and fall. One particularly useful feature is a set of plates showing the under-tail patterns. These views can help you distinguish among warblers, and may be the best you will get of a bird high in a tree. It may seem a bit voyeuristic, but it's really OK. Honest!

On a hopeful note, it is not really all that hard to learn to identify the warblers that return to your area year after year. Like the faces of your friends, they become recognizable after you have put a plumage to a name several times. And when they become familiar you begin to pick out the defining characteristics pretty

5. Taxonomy: the classification of animals and plants into scientifically sound categories. In the case of birds, it relates to their genus and species.
6. This book does not fit the definition of a field guide used in *Birding Lite.*

readily. The "old shoes" in my area are particularly simple:

- The Yellow-rumped Warbler has... well, you know.
- I call the Townsend's Warbler the Lone Ranger bird – again, pretty obvious.
- The Wilson's Warbler is bright yellow, wears a tiny black cap, and makes a unique yapping sound.

But be careful – there may be other warblers whose appearance is just slightly different from your avian buddies, and you might miss identifying a rare vagrant if you are too casual about it.

Summary

If you really want to get good at bird identification, there are ways to improve your observation skills. Then you won't have to rely on others to help you learn new birds. But a lot of this requires really engaging your left brain and investing some study time. The *Advanced Birding* guide is an excellent place to start, and then you might want to branch out to some of the group-specific books (either the ones mentioned here, or others). Create a plan – execute the plan.

But who says you have to get good at bird identification? A perfectly wonderful time can be had without your ever becoming proficient at separating out these difficult groups of birds. You will learn and grow as a birder just by watching birds, and there is nothing wrong with tagging along with knowledgeable, but not-too-serious, birders. So if you don't want to get all left-brainy, don't. After all, it is all about enjoying what you do. Some people get tremendous satisfaction from rising to the challenge of identifying every bird they see, while others would rather just go out and enjoy birds. It is your choice.

Remember. You are reading a book about birding because birds have really captured your imagination. The words below, written by John Burroughs in 1897, sum up a lot of my feelings about birds, and maybe they speak to you as well.

"The birds link themselves to your memory of seasons and places, so that a song, a call, a gleam of color, set going a sequence of delightful reminiscences in your mind. When a solitary great Carolina wren came one August day and took up its abode near me and sang and called and warbled as I had heard it long before on the Potomac, how it brought the old days, the old scenes back again, and made me for the moment younger by all those years!"

Weird-Bird

Birds are flyin' south for winter.
Here's the Weird-Bird headin' north,
Wings a-flappin', beak a-chatterin',
Cold head bobbin' back 'n' forth.
He says, "It's not that I like ice
Or freezin' winds and snowy ground.
It's just sometimes it's kind of nice
To be the only bird in town.

... Shel Silverstein

chapter ten

Hit the Books!
Continuing Education

> *"Some books are to be tasted, others to be swallowed, and some few to be chewed and digested: that is, some books are to be read only in parts, others to be read, but not curiously, and some few to be read wholly, and with diligence and attention."*
> Sir Francis Bacon

The above quotation is a perfect description of the universe of books and other resources for birders. And the variety is a good thing. Once the word gets out that you have more than a passing interest in birds, friends and family will instantly have gift ideas for you, the person who has everything. The vast majority of these gifts will fall into the first category – to be tasted. But there is nothing to keep you from dropping a few hints about resources that you would really like to own – the ones you could chew and digest to nourish your birding prowess. A few well-placed remarks might prevent your having to say, "You really shouldn't have." – and mean it! To enjoy a real feast, however, (to continue Bacon's metaphor) you may need to "pick up the tab" yourself.

The following categories are arbitrary, but they encompass just about every birding reference known to birderkind in North America. (Note that I have resisted using the "proper" form of citation I learned for high school term papers back in the Dark Ages. It is now easy to find a book without the name of the publisher's city mentioned.)

Field Guides of North American Birds

Chapter five described this group of books in detail. Some of the more highly-regarded field guides are:

- *Sibley Field Guide to Birds of North America*
- *Peterson Field Guide to Birds of North America*
- *Kaufman Field Guide to Birds of North America*
- *National Geographic Field Guide to Birds of North America*

Some of these come in regional issues – western, eastern, or central. Another field guide that is worth considering because of its easy-to-carry narrow shape is *All the Birds of North America: American Bird Conservancy's Field Guide* by Griggs.

Although they don't really qualify as field guides, there are a number of guide books for people (like my wife) who just can't tolerate the organization of a *bona fide* field guide. Some people have this irrational belief that there ought to be something logical about non-fiction books. So there are, for example, bird guides that are arranged by color. What a concept! One such book is the *Beginner's Guide to Birds* by Donald and Lillian Stokes (available in a number of versions, by region or not).

Another type of bird-identification aide is a book that actually plays the sounds of birds. Chapter two discusses some of the shortcomings of these books. But if you want to try one, you can Google "bird sound book."

And now we have the non-book field guide. As of this writing, you have a choice of at least three different "apps" that purport to give you a full field guide, with the advantage of audio, to North American birds on your smart phone. As this area is virtually exploding, whatever I would tell you about it here is bound to be obsolete by the time you read this.

Regional Birding Guides

These books tell about the birds you might find in a certain area. They can be useful if you are planning a trip (or relocating) to a particular area, e.g., the Gulf Coast or the Rocky Mountains. They usually do not contain the same level of detail as a field guide, but they give you an idea of what each bird you are likely to find there looks like. Your best bet is to search for these books on the web, or find them at a bookstore or bird store at your destination. Of course, these books are not just for North America – you can get one for your trip to Ecuador, too.

Books that provide detailed information about bird prevalence and dispersion, like Roberson's *Monterey Birds*, mentioned in the Local Resources section of chapter five, might be considered a subset of this category.

Books on Bird Groups/Families
Books on gulls, warblers, and sparrows were mentioned in chapter nine. The following is by no means an exhaustive list:
- Peterson Guide, *Gulls of the Americas*, by Howell and Dunn
- Peterson Guide, *Warblers*, by Dunn and Garrett
- *A Guide to the Identification and Natural History of the Sparrows of the United States and Canada*, by Rising and Beadle
- *Sparrows of the United States and Canada: The Photographic Guide*, by Beadle and Rising

Guides are also available for a number of other bird groups, including sea and coastal birds, shorebirds, raptors, owls, and hummingbirds.

Books on Bird Behaviors
There are four different types of books that fit in this category.
- *The Birder's Handbook*, by Ehrlich, Dobkin, and Wheye (described in chapter five and cited several times in this book), provides a comprehensive summary of key behaviors for nearly every North American bird.

- The *Stokes Guide to Bird Behavior* provides more detailed information on 75 species (in three volumes). Amazon.com lets you (at this writing) take a peek inside each volume to see which birds are covered and what kind of information is included about each.
- A number of books have been published about specific aspects of bird behavior, such as nesting, migration, songs, etc.
- If you are blessed with a keen sense of curiosity, *Bird Tracks and Sign*, by Elbroch and Marks, can help you identify birds by what they leave behind – tracks, feathers, nests, droppings, and other things.

Guides to Birdwatching Sites

These books tell you where the good birding places are in certain areas. For example, during a vacation to the southeastern states my birding was greatly facilitated by a book that told me about the nature preserves that attract great birds, which birds are likely to congregate there, and at what time of year. It was a big help in planning my itinerary and constructing my target bird list, enabling me to add over 30 birds to my life list. As with area-specific field guides, you are most likely to find one that fits your needs on the web. If you don't want to study ahead, you can also try a local birding emporium near your destination.

Books on Birding Techniques

Ahem! You are holding one! A few others are listed below and mentioned in chapter one, but don't limit yourself to just these – there are plenty on the market.
- *Sibley's Birding Basics*, by David Sibley (who else?) If you have read this far and still feel clueless but really want to become a competent birder, you should try Sibley's book next.
- *Bird Watching for Dummies*, by Bill Thompson III (In my humble opinion, if you watch birds you are, by definition, not a dummy, unless you have some other quirk that qualifies you.)

- *Bird Watching 101: The Ultimate Beginners Guide to Bird Watching* by Randall Magwood. A subtitle is, "Everything You Need To Know To Watch And Observe Birds *Properly*" (emphasis added). As you can probably tell, I am not big on propriety. But if you are a proper New Englander, this might be the book for you.
- National Geographic *Birding Essentials*, by Jonathan Alderfer and Jon Dunn.
- *Pete Dunne on Bird Watching: The How-to, Where-to, and When-to of Birding.*

Chapter seven discusses a book about a very specific birding technique – pishing. That book is *The Art of Pishing: How to Attract Birds by Mimicking Their Calls* by Pete Dunne.

Advanced Birding Guides
The best book I have found is the one mentioned in chapter nine, *Advanced Birding*, by Kenn Kaufman.

Specialty Books
Lots of books, including coffee table books, fit in this category. If there is any aspect of birdism that interests you, there is probably a book about it. Among the topics are:
- Bird Behavior
- Bird Photography
- Building Birdhouses
- Bird-friendly Gardens
- Bird Names
- Bird Nests

Resources to Help You Keep a Life List
This category includes books, software, and the Internet. Life-list books range from a simple checklist to fancy hard-bound books with photographs and a place to write a story about your first encounter with each bird. I am still using that beautiful *Audubon Life•List Journal*, published by the National Audubon Society, that got me started as a lister. I can't imagine switching to something else.

Since most of you are much younger than I, you may prefer to keep your life-list electronically. Can't blame you for that. A database of birds can make it easy to look up a bird, put your sightings in chronological order, analyze the locations of your first sightings, and do all those unnecessary things that people like to do. Knock yourself out. There are web sites that will keep your list for you, software you can load on your computer, bird identification software with a listing feature, and (undoubtedly) an "app" for your smart phone. In fact, by the time you read this, some brand new electronic marvel may have been developed that has an application for just this purpose.

Taking it to the Next Level
There is a profusion of books about birds and bird lovers – some a bit nutty. You are going to get books like these given to you – you can count on it. But in case you would like to get the jump on a friend or family-member who is a birder, here are a few titles:
- *Why Don't Woodpeckers Get Headaches?* by Mike O'Connor
- *Bird Brain-Teasers: Puzzles, Games & Avian Trivia*, by Patrick Merrill
- *Bill Oddie's Little Black Bird Book*
- *To See Every Bird on Earth*, by Dan Koeppel
- *The Big Year: A Tale of Man, Nature, and Fowl Obsession*, by Mark Obmascik
- *Birding on Borrowed Time*, by Phoebe Snetsinger
- *Life List*, by Olivia Gentile

Where do you go to acquire all these gems? Clearly, there are a myriad of places, including independent book sellers, book megastores, museum and park gift shops, and, of course, the web. But in my opinion, you would do well to locate a bird specialty store such as Wild Bird Center or Wild Birds Unlimited if there is one within a reasonable distance from your home. The above list was compiled mostly from data gathered at a visit to the Wild Bird Center in my area.

Friendly people there, and my guess is that you would find the same at the one near you, too.

In addition to a myriad of items for birders and people who just love birds, most bird emporiums have a very nice collection of books, pocket reference cards, tapes, CDs, DVDs, and other useful items especially for birders. There you are unlikely to need to choose between one field guide and no field guide. There you can actually open them up and see what it looks like inside – a nice (but disappearing) way of selecting a book. And you get to support a real, red-blooded local merchant.

You might have better luck finding some types of books by surfing the web. For example, your local bird emporium's collection probably doesn't have a guide to the birdwatching sites on the other side of the country. And you are going to have a better chance of finding a guide to the birds of a certain area at a store in that area.

We have come to the end of our little journey together through the wonderful land of birderdom. It was nice to have you along. I hope you found the journey comfortable, enlightening, entertaining, and beneficial. If you joined me to find out if birding is your cup of tea, I would like to be the first to welcome you into this joyous recreational pastime. One lump or two? If you already considered yourself a birder when you boarded this conveyance, I hope you learned a few new things that will help you to maximize your enjoyment while communing with our feathered friends. Perhaps we will meet out on the birding trails.

"Those little nimble musicians of the air, that warble forth their curious ditties, with which nature hath furnished them to the shame of art."

...Izaak Walton